FISHING BY MAIL

FISHING
BY MAIL

The Outdoor Life of a Father and Son

VANCE BOURJAILY
AND PHILIP BOURJAILY

THE ATLANTIC MONTHLY PRESS
NEW YORK

Atlantic Monthly Press
841 Broadway
New York, NY 10003

Published in Canada by General Publishing Company, Ltd.

Grateful acknowledgment is made to
the University of Oklahoma Press to quote from
Canadian River Hunt by General William
E. Strong. Copyright © 1960 by the University
of Oklahoma Press.

Library of Congress Cataloging-in-Publication Data

Bourjaily, Vance Nye.
    Fishing by mail: the outdoor life of a father and son / Vance
Bourjaily and Philip Bourjaily.—1st ed.
    ISBN 0-87113-556-6
    1. Bourjaily, Vance Nye—Correspondence.   2. Bourjaily, Philip—
Correspondence.   3. Authors, American—20th century—
Correspondence.   4. Fishers—United   States—Correspondence.
5. Outdoor life—United States.   I. Bourjaily, Philip.   II. Title.
PS3503.O77Z483   1993
799.1′092′2—dc20   93-6611

Manufactured in the United States of America
Designed by Debbie Glasserman
First Edition 1993
1   3   5   7   9   10   8   6   4   2

For Charles Bourjaily

Acknowledgments

———

Most of the people we need to thank are mentioned in the introductions to the three sections of the book. An exception is our agent, Michael Carlisle. Another is our editor, Bryan Oettel, who helped shape this book into more than just a pile of rambling correspondence. Thanks too to his successor, Bonnie Levy.

My personal thanks to Tim Thompson of the Iowa DNR, for bringing wild turkeys back to Old Man's Creek.—V.B.

I also need to thank Pam, who gave up the comforts of suburbia for the hardships of life in rural Iowa as an outdoor writer's wife. Without her generous help with everything from child care to line editing, my half of this book quite simply could not have been written.—P.B.

Contents

Introduction

___

This is an introduction not to this book but to my son, collaborator, and—in some of the exchanges—good-humored adversary, whose name, of course, is Philip. It is also an introduction to Redbird Farm, where Philip grew up and I (good humoredly, I like to think) helped raise him.

I'll slip myself in alongside Philip, here and there, in something like the way one puts a camera on a tripod, sets the self-timer, and runs around to stand beside the other subject, slightly out of breath.

Philip is almost thirty-five, which makes him a year or two less than half my age. I'll hit seventy before this sees print, and I guarantee I'll hit it as hard as I can. But look: If I can slide through ten more years, then he'll be more than half my age, and all I have to do is make it thirty-some more to see what he looks like as an old gentleman.

It's been some time, now, since Philip and I lived in the same region, let alone the same state or the same house. When I was still in Iowa, he was mostly in Barcelona, Spain, or Charlottesville, Virginia. He got back to Iowa about the time I left it for Arizona, first, and later Louisiana. So we never really got to hunt and fish together much. There's some reminiscing in the letters that follow about the times we did, but mostly our companionship in the field and stream has been by correspondence. Hence this book.

Philip is married to Pam, and they have a son called Chipper who is 1/23rd my age. They live near Homestead, Iowa, fifteen or twenty miles from Redbird Farm. They also have a dog, a German shorthair named Sam. I had a dog until sometime last year, a non-sporting, generic sort of family dog named Marigold. Philip said in one of his letters: "Sam wants to know what kind of a name is Marigold for a dog?"

I'll digress: The reason I had to yield Marigold—to a nice lady who lives in New Orleans named Sheryl—is that my second wife works in Miami. When she moved there from Baton Rouge, she moved into a no-dogs joint, at which I appear a couple of times a month. I live and work in Baton Rouge, where my job is college professing, which gives me a lot of vacation days to spend in Miami, too. There wasn't much in Baton Rouge for my energetic, Indian-born, city-loving wife. Her father was chief inspector of police in Bombay while she was growing up; he makes an appearance as the book goes on.

Not being able to take Marigold back and forth to Miami, and she not being the sort to settle happily into a kennel and wait (what she is is an intense, part Border collie who climbs any fences she can't jump), I took to leaving Marigold with the above-mentioned Sheryl. They adored one another, so I made Marigold a gift to Sheryl.

Last time I saw Sheryl and inquired, a bit wistfully, about my former dog, Sheryl said, sweet and shy:

"I gave her a birthday party."

"You did? How did you know when her birthday was?"

"I decided it was April twentieth. We had ice cream and cake."

"Were there guests?"

"We had two other dogs," Sheryl said.

Got that, Shorthair Sam? They probably had party hats, too.

End digression. Back to Philip: The guy's education began conventionally enough, in the public schools of Iowa City, where I was teaching in those years. Going into his sophomore year, I got a sabbatical and a grant, and we spent the school year in Barcelona.

In the British school in that sometimes elegant Catalonian city, Philip found a man who could do for him something no one could ever do for his father: teach him math. The next year Philip chose to leave us behind in Iowa and go back to the math man. My son boarded with friends. He went back again his senior year, boarded with a Spanish family, became bilingual, learned that my paella was not altogether authentic, and gave up math for beer.

But let me turn back to that sophomore year, when I learned something interesting, too. During much of it we had a pale-blue-collar, maybe verging on junior executive, apartment. Philip's mother and younger sister, Robin, had gone back to Iowa after Christmas, and I was doing the Barcelona cooking and housekeeping and punching away at a novel.

I've always enjoyed cooking (Philip does, too); I loved shopping in the big, open-air market, and up till then I'd thought of cleaning and tidying as drudgery. But it's mindless stuff. You can make a bed and mop the kitchen and be thinking about whatever it is you want to think about, probably your stubborn novel.

Cooking interferes if you must do it not just on impulse or occasion, but day in, day out. You've got to think about what to cook, go shop for the stuff, do the kitchen part. If you don't concentrate and put what happens to the bird-watcher's buddy in the next chapter out of your mind, your paella's going to be worse than inauthentic. So I came to prefer the drudgery.

Let me illustrate. Philip's soccer coach and a classmate are coming to dinner. The coach is called Mick, played the English equivalent of Triple A pro ball, and is tough and active. When he comes in with the guys after soccer practice on a chilly afternoon, there'll be three hungry athletes to feed, and it's going to take paella to fill them up. So I stop writing early to have time for the market, which closes in the afternoon so folks can get away for the big noon meal and the sometimes sensuous siesta.

In the market I stop at the stall of a particular chicken lady I fancy because I think she fancies me, not that I'm a candidate for her siesta list. She's pudgy but jolly, and when I say, "Paella," she starts to shuffle chickens. Speaking in Catalan, she makes what must be a bawdy joke with the word "American" in it to the chicken lady in the next stall, and they both break up. Meanwhile, the right chicken has been selected and is getting cut up into bite-sized pieces with a pair of mounted scissors about three times the size of tin snips.

I move on with it, get a nice, garlicky chorizo from the sausage lady, and about two-thirds of a pound of pork loin from a butcher lady (only we don't do it in pounds and ounces—here it's 300 grams, *trescientos gramos*). I need a good, big, red onion—garlic I've got at home—and a sweet red pepper, and plenty of saffron. Having plenty of saffron makes me feel like a rich man.

I buy four plump plum tomatoes, *trescientos gramos* of fresh peas, a small cauliflower, of which I'll use half, and half a dozen very small artichokes. There are oyster mushrooms. I get a few. Having saved the best for last, I go into the seafood part of the market.

In the market, the meats and poultry are commonplace to look at, the charcuterie stuff interesting in its variety, the fruits and vegetables quite beautiful, but the seafood is visually intoxicating. Seventy-five, eighty stalls of gleaming fish and shellfish, every color: black, wonderfully ugly monkfish, the flounder family in all its sizes with both eyes together on the same side, fish that are red, pink, blue, purple, yellow—how they glisten, and how the shellfish shine in their surreal shapes.

Today it's shellfish for me. I buy a dozen medium shrimp, a

dozen hard-shell clams, two dozen mussels, and I'm in luck—even if there were lobsters, my pale-blue-collar self couldn't afford them, no matter how much saffron I own—but look, my seafood queen has *cigales*. A little pedantry coming now: *cigales* in Spanish, *langoustines* in French, and Dublin Bay prawns in English. These are what you should get when you order *scampi* in an Italian restaurant in the States, but you won't. You'll get large shrimp, which will be good, but they won't be *scampi*. The real ones are large, saltwater crawfish, sort of—no, they're *cigales*. They are terrific, and there in Barcelona, expecting Mick, Peter, and Philip to dinner, I scoop up eight of the beauties. The bird-watcher's buddy can wait till tomorrow.

Back in the apartment I break up the cauliflower into florets, shell the peas, and reduce the little artichokes to hearts, squeezing some lemon juice on them so they won't go brown on me. I clean the mussels, snap off the heads of the *cigales* and shrimp, and cut the sausage and pork into slices and cubes. There is stomping on the stairs. I put out the red jug-wine for the athletes. We'll be eating in about half an hour.

I use a big skillet and a smaller one, pouring olive oil into both. In the big one I toss chopped onion and garlic, cauliflower and artichoke hearts, while the pork sausage and chicken bites brown in the other. Then into the big skillet I sprinkle three cups of long grain rice and let it sizzle until it starts getting transparent. Next I add the meats, and six cups of boiling water into which I've put a teaspoon of my precious saffron thread, pulverized in a mortar.

Now comes the inauthenticity. I don't own, and don't much want to, a *paella*, which is a long, shallow oval pan with a handle at each end, and into which I ought to put what's cooking, and the rest of the ingredients, preparatory to slipping it into the oven.

But I like the control of keeping this project on top of the stove. When it's simmering away, and the rice is about half done, I put in the clams and mussels and sliced red peppers. If I were using lobster, this would be the time for claws and tails, but of course I'm not. When the rice in the big skillet is moist and yellow, and the grains have separated, I add the shrimp, the mushroom slices, the shelled peas, the *cigale* tails, and a bunch of capers. Now it all cooks together until the rice is gleaming and ready, and I put the skillet on the table, along with a dish of *espinaca catalána* (cook some spinach halfway; cook some bacon till crisp, and cook chopped onions, garlic, pine nuts, and raisins in the fat; add the spinach, crumble the bacon up in it; yum).

Anyway, I serve these things to the soccer players and their coach, and for a while there is the silence of men seriously dining, interrupted by the grunts of the same men seriously wining. Then Coach Mick looks at me and says softly:

"Hell of a paella, Dad."

The last time I heard anything like this kind of reverence in his voice was during a soccer game in which Philip was playing fullback. Philip is already a big kid to five-foot-seven eyes; he's six feet tall at sixteen, new to soccer, and I'd have expected him to play it tentatively. But in this game, as the opponent's striker came dribbling fast toward the goal, with the goalie out of position and Philip the last man in the way, my dumb kid does a maneuver that looks like a baseball player trying to break his leg sliding into a third baseman. But what Philip is sliding into is the soccer ball, and, plowing grass with his back, he hooks it, and the striker, too, who goes butt over bumblebee. Goal saved, and Mick, from the sidelines, jumps up and down and shouts:

"Hell of a tackle, son."

Philip and I were pretty close that year in Barcelona, and I say that preliminary to reporting on an area in which we were greatly different. At home, we never hunted together. Philip, as a boy and an adolescent, didn't have any killing in him.

He was a strong, joyful, athletic kid who played both ways

on his eighth-grade football team, making blocks and tackles as punishing as anyone else's. He was a good, natural shot with a shotgun, which I am not, and would enjoy outshooting me on clay. He just didn't want to kill stuff. We did some fishing together, about which some reminiscing is about to begin, and Philip was fond of eating fish—the ones I caught. The ones he caught, he threw back.

Philip is now, as you will learn from the second section of this book, a dedicated hunter, of both deer and birds, and I will read with interest his introduction to that section, hoping to learn the answer to something that has puzzled me a lot: How and why did the change take place?

In college, at the University of Virginia, Philip became thoroughly practical: with no interest in going to graduate school, he majored in art history, a field in which there are zero jobs for anyone short of a Ph.D. And he rowed crew, a sport that not only offered no scholarships, but also one in which the oarsmen had to split expenses themselves when they competed out of town—gas, lodging, and enormous meals.

Since then he's become, as noted, a hunter. He and Pam and Chipper live in a farmhouse in good pheasant country, and Pam is a Ph.D. candidate in English lit. Philip, building on his solid foundation in rowing and art history, has begun a career. He writes for the outdoor magazines: *Sports Afield, Field and Stream, American Hunter,* and so on. I once did some of that kind of writing for a couple of those magazines, but more often for the *New Yorker* and *Esquire* back in the sixties. But I wasn't working on a career in the field; I was putting together chapters for a hunting book called *The Unnatural Enemy,* the only one of my twelve books, most of them novels, currently in print. (The University of Arizona Press reissued it and keeps it going in a modest way.) In time, I drifted away from outdoor writing, but Philip is apparently getting a reputation in the field.

I'll tell you what else he's getting: bald. Like me. Once,

when I was his age, I was on an archaeological dig in Mexico that was being filmed, as most are. And one morning the cameraman was up above us on a particularly steep hill, as we climbed up toward him. When you watched the picture you saw hat crowns coming toward you, bandannas, bare heads, and I saw this guy coming who had no hair at all on the crown of his skull and wondered which of us it was, and it was me. When Philip wears a beard, as he sometimes does, and as I would except that it makes my face itch, he has more hair on his chin than he does on the top of his head.

Philip grew up on the farm.

It's called Redbird Farm. I lived there fifteen years. I miss it.

West of Des Moines, Iowa flattens out into what once were the prairies, but Redbird Farm is well east of Des Moines, and hilly. It's about five hundred acres of timber, pasture, and creek bottom. Some of the bottomland could be farmed in row crops, but Old Man's Creek floods rather often and the crops are lost. So Redbird Farm includes most of the land along the Black Diamond Road that the professional farmers didn't want. We liked it that way.

While I was there we built three good-sized ponds: the upper pond, the lower pond, and the woods pond. Now there's a seven-acre duck marsh, too, where corn was once grown; the marsh must thrive on the flooding.

The timber is mixed hardwood—white and red oak, hickory, walnut, and ash. There's a small farmhouse down beside the road. In nineteenth-century Iowa the roads were marked by symbols rather than numbers. The Black Diamond, the Red Ball. They were stagecoach roads.

Up a steep hill, on the way to the timber, is what was formerly a one-room school. It, too, was beside the road when we bought the farm, but we moved it up the hill a couple of hundred yards and built the final pond, a small one for swimming, nearby. The schoolhouse has huge north windows, and a view across the pastures, over the timber and into the distance; it was my writing place for all those years.

The woods and pastures support a lot of squirrels and rabbits; there are pheasants in the fields, and though it's not a hot spot for them, a covey or two of quail. Ducks use the ponds intermittently. One fall the local wood ducks decided to use the woods pond as their local rallying point, from which to start the migration. I heard them before I saw them, and crawled to a sheltered place on the bank to count. I stopped counting at around a hundred; there were lots more. I crawled away so as not to disturb them.

And one spring when the bottomland flooded, a pair of migrant swans stayed a week, and there was a bald eagle finding carrion fish in the shallow part.

Philip's mother still lives on the farm. There are sheep, cattle, and horses, in smaller numbers now than formerly, and deer and squirrels in larger numbers than formerly.

When Kurt Vonnegut came to teach at Iowa one fall, I remember taking him for a walk through the woods, and around the ponds. I was bitching, as we came to the upper pond, about income taxes, and Kurt said, "What do you expect? You've got your own state park."

One more thing about paella: it doesn't matter if you can't get all the ingredients. Once I was visiting a Moslem household where pork wasn't eaten. Made them a paella with turkey sausage and pastrami, along with the chicken and shellfish. Worked out, as most things do if you can get your mind around them, pretty well.

PART ONE

FISHING BY MAIL

While Philip and I were living in Barcelona, I decided one weekend to drive across Spain to the northeastern corner, to visit the city of Pamplona, where much of Hemingway's *The Sun Also Rises* is set—and where, in a different season of the year, the youth of Europe still comes to run through the streets in front of the bulls that will be fought that afternoon.

The bulls are released at the railroad station, the streets are barricaded, and the young people run between the barricades into the bullring, with the bulls charging along after them.

Perhaps if my purpose in going had been for that ritual, Philip would have wanted to go along, but since what I wanted was to have a quiet look at the town and then perform a certain ritual of my own having to do with trout fishing, he declined. He'd have gone if I'd urged him, we both think now (and he wishes I had), but he was seventeen, and there were friends and parties for him that weekend, back in Barcelona.

The town, which has a bronze statue of Hemingway, still has, as well, at least two of the spots in which the characters from *The Sun* caroused, the Cafe Uruña and Montoya's Hotel. But it has Roman ruins, too; it was founded by Pompey, back in Caesar's time, and the founder called it after himself, Pompeyopolis, which the Moors corrupted to Pamplona.

I'm not sure Philip had read Hemingway's novel at the time. It certainly didn't have the resonance for him it had for me, nor is there any reason why it should have. So the fishing ritual wouldn't have meant much to him, particularly since I was pretty sure there wouldn't be much action beyond my odd, literary nostalgia. But back in the early 1920s, fifty years earlier, Hemingway's characters, Jake and Bill, toward whom my nostalgia was directed, had found good fishing by traveling the route I now followed. It began in Pamplona. Jake and Bill took the bus from there, riding with wine-drinking Basques to the Pyrenees-mountain village of Burguete. I went up in a Hertz rental hatchback.

When Jake and Bill checked in to the inn at Burguete, it was very cold, and Bill immediately started playing the upright piano in the salon to keep warm. I'd have played the same piano, which is still there, but it was locked. I didn't need it for warmth, anyway.

In the morning, before breakfast, I did as Jake does in the book: walked down to a brook behind the inn. He dug worms there, but I decided I'd fish with flies, as Bill did. The breakfast menu hadn't changed—buttered toast, coffee, and raspberry jam. The innkeeper's cook packed a lunch for me, as her predecessor had for my guys, and I walked off with the lunch and a bottle of wine in my backpack, rod case slung over my shoulder and fly box in my pocket. I had a couple of McGintys in it, a fly that looks like a little bee. Bill's fly.

I opened the geodetic survey map I'd bought for the trip and took my bearings on the huge old abbey of Roncevaux, high above me in the mountain pass where Charlemagne got whipped a thousand years ago and Roland died. It was easy, then, to find the path from Hemingway's description.

It was a cool morning. The ground was damp and spongy underfoot. The trees were small, as I knew they'd be from Hemingway's description of his own, similar nostalgia trip, made after *The Sun Also Rises* was published and had brought him great fame. He'd found the great old first-growth beech trees of Jake and Bill's hike all cut down, and the streams unshaded. Since then, it seemed, the second growth must have been harvested, too, probably for firewood.

It was a long walk, and a pleasant one, but there were no trout in the Río de la Fábrica. *Fábrica* means factory, and the shell of what was once a munitions factory still stands there. But the dam under which Jake fished in the book, and which must have supplied power for the factory, has been torn out. The stream is too shallow for fish, and too warm. Only the spring-box, where Jake and Bill put their wine, is, oddly enough, still there. I put my jug in the same place and walked on downstream, Bill's route, not even trying to fish until I came to the main branch of a much larger river, the Irati, into which the Río de la Fábrica empties.

And there, standing on a big rock, I caught a trout. I tried one of the McGintys first, of course, but there were no rising fish, and it didn't look like dry-fly water. Then I tried with something called a Hornberg Special, tied for me back home by my friend John Yount (whom I'll be introducing soon), dressed with lemon feathers from a wood duck. Lemon feathers. Many pages along from here, Philip will send me some more of them, to send to John.

The Irati River trout went for the Hornberg wet, but she didn't hit it very hard. I could barely feel her suck it in.

She was a small brown, not long out of the hatchery. Her color hadn't brightened yet from being free. I put her back. Then damned if I didn't have an adventure.

I was restless when I got back to my hatchback, in spite of the long hike, and wanted to do something strenuous. Driving around, I saw, above some mountain village with a forest on both edges, the result of a gigantic rock slide—acres and acres of tumultuous, jagged black rocks, six to eight feet high. As if a choppy sea had turned to granite.

The villagers warned me against walking across it, so, of

course, once I got out of their sight, I walked, jumping and scrambling from rock to rock like a nutty kid, tearing my shoes up.

About two thirds of the way across, I saw a nest, a big one, eight or ten feet wide, built down in the rocks. It was beautifully protected and concealed, except from my particular angle, and had rushes for sides and soft plant material for a lining.

I climbed down and over to look inside, and the nest was full of wild piglets, wonderful, strange, soft little striped creatures, a pound or two each. The young of a wild boar. I was nervous and delighted. If Mama's around . . . , I thought, and scrambled off, clumsy and exhilarated. The secret was safe with me. I had no intention of going back to tell the friendly Basques in the village that there was something up here fellows might want to haul away in a sack to raise and barbeque.

I'm not sure how much of this I told Philip at the time, back in Barcelona, so I thought I'd write it for him now, as well as for whatever readers we may win, because it becomes a paradigm for much of the section I'm introducing.

(Hey, readers, I apologize for *paradigm*, which is merely a fancy word for *pattern*. Trying to win you, I don't want to lose you with stuff like that, so I'd better explain myself. Last summer my sometimes-contentious wife took a graduate course in which the fancier word was used by teacher and students as if it were the final key to all knowledge. So I thought I'd send it back to its old, simple meaning one time, and if you'll forgive me for it, I'll let you in on a really great and fancy word I found when I checked the spelling. How about *paralamdacism*? It means the inability to pronounce the letter *l*, something with which I was comically afflicted at the age of about five. Lions were *yions* and lambs were *yams* and, okay, I'll try to get back in *yine*.)

The pattern I'm speaking of sets in once Philip and I are done reminiscing in the fishing stuff that's coming. After that,

I start writing to him from various far places. He can't do much in his letters except cheer me on, any more than I can do much except cheer him on when, in the second section, he becomes a hunter in Iowa for wild turkeys. Reason for the book, I guess. Letters as a way of sharing experiences we aren't able to have, in the manner of some fathers and sons, together.

Now for some introductions:

Among the people mentioned in the book are the Lardners. Dek is a very old friend, a surgeon now living in Illinois with whom I used to hunt ducks when he was doing his residency in Iowa City. Dek has four children, three of them sons around Philip's age. Philip became friends with all three boys, and we five took a fine fishing trip together, which is about to be related. My role in that one was not always stellar.

John, who is going to take me fishing for landlocked salmon in the second chapter, is John Yount, a phenomenal novelist and phenomenal fisherman. Art, in that chapter, is an orthopedist and John's regular fishing companion.

In the saltwater fishing pieces, I think I pretty much identify people as they come along, except for Dave Wilson, whom Philip already knows. Dave was a student of mine once (as was John, actually, but much longer ago), has published some fiction, and works hard at writing more of it. He makes his living as a financial planner, when he isn't working on fishing boats. He was doing the second of those things as a mate on one of the times I've written about, but has his captain's license now, and I recommend him. I can't say whether his financial plans are any better than anyone else's, but he'll get you into fish. Try the Miami phone book. It's Wilson, David B.

One David to go, David Seybold, editor of sporting anthologies, who, as you'll see in the very first letter in chapter one, got Philip and me started on our correspondence. Nice fellow, and we thank him for pushing us in.

Chapter 1

FISHING BY MAIL

New London, NH

April 16, 1986

Mr. Philip Bourjaily
Homestead, Iowa

Dear Philip,

I trust you are well and enjoying spring . . . Would you be interested in writing a story for an anthology I am editing? It is to be called *Seasons of the Angler* . . . What I would really like, to be perfectly honest, is a story by you *and* your father . . . one story penned by father and son would be unique and extremely enlightening.

Please read the enclosed material and let me know what you think. . . .

Sincerely,
David Seybold

(From the enclosed material)
"My foremost objective is to provide insights into the character of the angler in today's society . . . what his act

8

of fishing means to him—and what he thinks it means to the society in which he lives."

. . .

Homestead, IA

Dear Dad,

I received this intriguing surprise in the morning mail. Not being the introspective sort, I have never given much thought to my place in society as a fisherman. Looking back over the years for some clue, all I can remember is falling into a lot of rivers, breaking several rod tips, not catching very many fish, and, on one famous occasion, hooking you in the nose with an errant backcast.

I don't know what I have learned from all this besides what a grown man with a trout fly stuck in his nose sounds like, nor do I see how I would have turned out differently if I'd spent my youth losing kites instead of fishing tackle in trees, but I'll give the matter quite a bit of thought.

Love,
Philip

. . .

Baton Rouge, LA

Dear Philip,

Like you I am ladled into a gentle stew of bemusement over the question of what our "act of fishing means to the society in which we live." On a scale of public nuisance to civic benefactor, we might be placed slightly higher than water-skiers, if measurably lower than professional clowns. As inadvertent clowns we do pretty well, as your letter reminds me, earning as much laughter when observed as, while giving less offense than, such brother amateurs as folksingers and guys who claim they know how to fix your car. We are probably about as neutral as stamp collectors, but I really don't know.

What I do know is the solution to our bafflement. Through

some years of intermittent engagement with attempts at writing thoughtful nonfiction, I've found, often enough, that thought won't crystallize and have learned to apply the following sneaky rule: *When in doubt, tell a story, reasonably true if possible.* Here is the reasonably true, particular story of my own earliest recollection of taking you fishing.

It was a Fourth of July weekend. You were three and a half. We went, with your mother and your older sister, to camp and fish for trout in northeast Iowa, where the limestone creeks once held native brook trout. When the banks were cleared, many years ago, the water temperatures went up and the brookie population went down. Now the creeks are suitable for put-and-take stocking of rainbows and browns.

I can't remember the name of the stream we camped by— to get there you go to Decorah, turn east, go a couple of miles, turn off south through pasture and woodland. Fishing starts at a stretch about seven miles from town.

We drove up beside the creek in a car track for a mile or so and put up our tent where the water fell in a series of shallow rock pools. Your sister and I strung up fly rods and walked downstream to a fairly deep hole, where Anna started fishing with a salmon egg and I tied on some wet fly or other. I'm going to guess it was a Queen of the Waters, which seems regally attractive to me, although I don't recall that many trout shared that opinion.

It was extremely hot. That water was low and clear. After an unproductive hour it occurred to me to dip a hand in the water. Even below the surface it felt lukewarm, nothing the fish would want to venture out into from whatever deep and shaded crannies they were basking in. I decided it was basking time for me, too, back at camp with a cold beer.

"It's too hot. The trout aren't active," I called out to your mother as we arrived. She was sitting on a rock, watching you and Moon, the weimaraner, play in a shallow pool.

"But Philip's got one," your mother said. "That's a trout, isn't it? Show Daddy."

Whereupon you held up a live, comatose 22-inch rainbow you were playing with, then plunged her back again into the tepid stream. The hatchery folks had stocked up heavily for the weekend. The place we'd stopped seemed to have been one of the stocking points, and along with the usual 7- to 12-inch fish, they'd apparently added one of the larger females, now retired from being inseminated and milked.

She was disoriented, I suppose, out of her hatchery tank, and overheated, with no residual instinct to tell her to swim away to coolness.

Yesterday afternoon, sitting in a big striped tent at the New Orleans Jazz Festival, eating barbecued alligator and listening to a woman named Carrie Smith sing a Bessie Smith blues song called "Just Give Me One More Smile," I couldn't lose the thought that we'd done right by that fat old lady trout—put her in a bucket and carried her to a deep hole where she might have found a cool place. I'm not sure we did that, I only hope we did. All I'm sure of is that she was the largest trout you or I ever caught.

Anyway, someone asked me what alligator tasted like, and I was able to tell her it's a whole lot like iguana.

Love,
Dad

. . .

Homestead, IA

Dear Dad,

I would have thought alligator tasted like snapping turtle, since they are both so bad tempered, but that just shows what a provincial guy I am. I do remember how that large rainbow trout tasted: like the doughballs the hatchery workers at Manchester throw into those long concrete troughs full of fish. I know because we ate that fish. Three-and-a-half-year olds don't always do the right thing by the fish they catch, but then neither do a lot of adults.

Of course, you didn't raise me to be a trout tickler, and I

believe it was shortly after that trip to Decorah that you took me to the tackle shop at Abercrombie & Fitch and bought me a four-foot bamboo fly rod and matching Hardy reel. Few children have received such auspicious starts to their fly-fishing careers, but I'm sure none of them has parlayed that advantage into baser incompetence than have I.

This is not to say I haven't had my fly-fishing moments. I have. Some of them have even involved catching fish, but the one I remember as most inspirational does not, at least on my part. We were on a family car trip, either en route to or returning from Boulder, Colorado, in 1969. Stopping at a large national park—I believe it was Rocky Mountain National Park—we parked at the first beaver pond and uncased our fly rods. Several people were arranged around the edge of the pond, sitting on camp chairs, watching bobbers unexpectantly. You and I began casting, which excited no little curiosity on the part of the assembled bait fishermen, particularly because my own style, while earnest, resembled a child defending himself from a swarm of buffalo gnats. Painfully aware that we were the center of attention, I yearned for the anonymity of a spin-casting rig and a hat less conspicuous than the jaunty Australian digger model with flies stuck in the band that I wore in those days. It was what theological types call a crisis of faith.

As if in answer, you caught a fish. Not a huge fish, just the sort of trout anglers other than myself pull routinely from western beaver ponds. To judge from the reaction of the other fishermen, however, it was a newsworthy event. Two teenagers who had been watching nearby came over to see your fish.

"Whadja catch him on?" asked one.

"This trout fly, son," you said, holding up a yellow and black McGinty for them to see. "You might want to find some smaller hooks for your night crawlers."

Someday, I thought, retrieving my own fly from a clutching willow, I'll be like that. Seventeen years later I have not yet lived up to the *beau ideal* of the gracious purist you set for me. I do most of my fishing now for bass and catch them on ugly rubber grubs.

The subject of bass is a melancholy one this year. We had a long, snowy winter, and when the ice melted off our farm pond in March, the wind blew a huge raft of winter-killed fish up along the dam. There were 4-pound bass, bluegills the size of Master Frisbees, and the walleyes we put in years ago and never saw again, all of them bigger than the largest bass. A couple of local tournament bass fishermen I know wanted to come out fishing even after I told them about the winterkill. Tom and John told me that if there were fish to be caught in the pond it was only a matter of figuring out how they were relating to the subsurface structure and then finding the right bait. I said glumly that as far as I knew the fish were relating to the structure by floating upside down over the top of it. After a long, unproductive morning they were ready to agree with me. We're going to catch some bass in a neighbor's pond and try restocking in a couple of weeks.

On a happier note, the morel mushrooms have come and gone in satisfying numbers, and Cousin Shaun bushwhacked a wild turkey after it flew down from its roost at the Hawkeye Wildlife Area just as shooting hours began. He smoked it and brought me a large piece of the breast, which tasted, no doubt, just like smoked alligator.

Love,
Philip

. . .

Baton Rouge, LA

Dear Philip:

This correspondence seems to deal as much with eating as it does with fishing, which is appropriate to the reminiscence I'm about to self-inflict. It goes back to our one grand fishing trip, to the Big Hole in Montana, with Dek Lardner and his boys. Distrustful that any hand but mine should turn the spatula, I appointed myself camp cook—well, motel cook. And I will maintain that I started off with a real triumph when I presented the first day's catch *flambé*, pouring a jigger of Wild Turkey over the hot fish as they came out from under the broiler, coated with butter, fennel, garlic, and slivered almonds. The flame when I lit a kitchen match not only astonished the company but was explosive enough to be satisfactorily alarming, and the trout (add lemon and Tabasco to taste) were absolutely great. As I hope you'll agree.

The next night we ate out. At noon on the third day I realized a fantasy. I had always felt one could cook *Truite au Bleu sur Rive*—I've probably got the preposition wrong, and maybe the final noun as well. It's supposed to mean Blue Trout Streamside and, grammar notwithstanding, the method should be known to all: 1. As you catch your trout, keep them alive. 2. Heat a large pot of water to boiling; add vinegar, salt, and small, peeled new potatoes. 3. When the potatoes are tender, remove the pot from heat. Quickly kill and gut the trout, dropping them into scalding water while they are still quivering. 4. In a couple of minutes, the skin separates, the flesh flakes and turns pale blue. 5. Remove, and serve fish and potatoes with butter, salt, and pepper. Best damn trout I ever cooked or ate (your agreement again seems necessary), and what could I do to exceed it?

Well, the sophisticated chef takes advantage of fresh local produce in season, and what Montana produces mostly is sagebrush. The trout presented on the evening of the fourth day were marinated in white wine and heaps of sage leaves, sautéed *meunière*, and rivaled the green persimmon in mouth-puckering ability. Jamie and David Lardner volunteered to run down to the corner for hamburgers, and I don't believe even the motel cats would touch the trout.

There was only one other low-comedy moment for me in

what was otherwise a very fine trip, and I don't think I've ever confessed this one. Jamie, Stephen, David, Dek, and you went off someplace arduous, and I elected to fish an easy stretch of water running through the next-door ranch all by myself. Looked good, and I felt lazy. Up to that hour we hadn't thought it would be practical to try to carry any fish back to Iowa, but here and now, it seemed to me, feasibility flickered. Whatever I might catch and clean I could hustle to the motel, pack in an ice chest, and it would reach Iowa with us five hours later. It was dusk, there was a hatch on, and I was motivated to fish hard. The hatch looked something like a #8 Irresistible, and I had one of those deer-hair beauties. I was on the shallow side of a very long, swirling pool, with a rock wall opposite, curves for concealment, nothing behind me, trout leaping in front. I cast to one, and now I had him, now I didn't. I hooked him fine, brought him halfway to where I stood in the stream and almost to the landing net before he flipped off. I did it again. It happened again. Fish caught, fish lost. In half an hour, I think I had 30 fish—a fish a minute—hit, take, and slip off. It was exciting, frustrating, and deeply puzzling. But no experienced angler will have to turn to some footnote at the end of this for a solution to the puzzle: Bourjaily *père* had neglected to check the hook on his beautiful #8 Irresistible. The point and barb were broken off.

While I was thus learning humility, I believe you were completing your famous Big Hole Hat Trick, but I have never heard the details of it, and I need now to know that tale of success, in order to restore family pride.

I brood about your winterkill. Each time it happened when I was on the farm, I'd question whether I really wanted to restock. But, well, our walleyes lasted seven years, and some of those bass must have been close to the same age. And there must be further measures—windmills, maybe hay bales floated just before freeze-up to keep air going in. As long as the ponds were there, it seemed to me we had to keep trying.

Love,
Dad

. . .

Homestead, IA

Dear Dad,

I'm sorry to contradict your total recall, but my memories of motel dining in Montana are a little different: The Lardners and I were so sick of trout after a solid week of it that we mutinied and bought a couple of chickens, which you then stuffed with sage when we weren't looking. The great suspense of the evening was provided by Dek Lardner, who was visibly on the brink of blurting the punchline to his favorite joke (you know, the one about the camp cook that ends: "This tastes like mooseflop pie—but *good!*") but, thanks to his excellent upbringing, did not.

It is true that I did complete the Big Hole Grand Slam or whatever it is they call it, catching each of five species of trout found in the river. The five are rainbow, brookie, cut-throat, brown, and grayling, and the Big Hole is the only river in the Lower 48 where all five can be found in the same place. While you were losing all those fish near the motel that day, the Lardner brothers and I drove several miles upstream to a place where the Big Hole, which was ex-tremely low that year, wound slowly through a pasture with some red cows in it. Except for the mountains in the back-ground it looked a great deal like the trout streams in north-east Iowa we used to fish.

David and Stephen moved on upstream to fish, and Jamie, who was bored with catching trout, went looking for rat-tlesnakes. I found a small pool that looked good to me, plopped a red Humpy into the current above it, and immediately caught a 10-inch rainbow. I cast back to the same place and found myself fast to a mountain whitefish, a species that apparently singled me out as being the only member of our party deserving of their attention on the trip. I caught another trout, then a whitefish, another trout, and so on. Noticing the Humpy was somewhat the worse for wear, I replaced it with a fresh one, made yet another cast to the head of the pool, and saw the surface dimple slightly around the fly, which was carried off daintily to the bottom. I set the hook with my customary finesse—it's the same motion as pull-starting a reluctant lawn mower, but with more feeling—and the battle was joined. I made short work of the fish with the heirloom Heddon the Lardners had lent me for the week, a phone-pole-stiff nine-and-a-half footer with checkered walnut grips. In five seconds the fish was swimming meekly at my feet. Neither trout nor whitefish, he was a beautiful purple-green fish with an oversized, flowing dorsal fin. Grayling, I realized, carefully unhooking the fly. I admired the fish and was relieved to see him swim away unhurt.

About this time David and Stephen rejoined me, creels bulging with large trout. I told them I'd caught a grayling. They looked at me blankly. I explained what it was. Stephen then said, "Oh, yeah, we caught a bunch of those upstream but we let 'em go. We thought they were suckers." Sic transit gloria piscatori.

Later, much later in fact, after we had locked the keys in the trunk of our rental car and recovered them by pulling out the backseat, we determined that I was the only member of our party to achieve the fabled Grand Slam. The margin of victory turned out to be a tiny cutthroat caught and released by me earlier in the week. Since there was no contest as to who had caught the fewest and smallest fish on the trip, I rarely brag about my accomplishments on the Big Hole, at least not to anyone who was there.

Tom and John came back to help me restock the pond a few days ago. Fishing was slow, and we caught only nine small bass among us. After a couple of hours I drove the fish back to our pond to release them. As I approached the water's edge, I noticed several bluegills finning in place just under the surface. They withdrew to a prudent distance and watched balefully as I dumped the bass into the pond, wondering who I was and why I was adding bigger fish to the food chain. The largemouths scattered blindly, heading for cover, and the alarmed bluegills turned together and disappeared as if sucked up by a vacuum cleaner.

So, some fish seem to have survived the winter after all, and two of the bass I released were full of eggs. Life will go on in the pond despite my heavy-handed stewardship. John told me the local B.A.S.S. club improves cover in lakes by wrapping chains around Christmas trees for ballast, then dragging them out onto the ice in the winter so they'll sink to the bottom and provide hiding places in the spring. Maybe I can try that.

Have a good summer in India. What do they fish for there, anyway?

Love,
Philip

．　．　．

London, England

Dear Philip,

Thank you for filling in the hole in the Big Hole, and I'm delighted to hear you have fish in the pond again. In answer to your question, the great freshwater game fish of India is the mahseer, for which I hope to be fishing next week. So far, no one here in London can tell me more than I already know, which is that the mahseer has the disposition of a very cross muskie and grows up to four feet in length and up to ninety-some pounds. According to the *Encyclopedia Britannica*, the mahseer is a barbel, and so related to the carp, but is most emphatically not a vegetarian. His "flesh, like that of the salmon, is much esteemed."

. . .

I have distilled my scant knowledge of the mahseer into the following verse:

> We're off to Kashmir, to catch the mahseer,
> Whose teeth are as sharp as a headhunter's spear.
> We will bait with live cobras to conquer our fear,
> And his much esteemed flesh we will eat with cold beer.

You and I have now, I judge, totally and irresponsibly evaded producing any insights into the role of the angler in today's society, but it's been fun writing. The fishing was fun, too—and why isn't that a pretty good insight right there? The fisherman finds enjoyment in a pursuit that is very close to harmless, more so than hunting since you can return the quarry undamaged by fishing barbless. You can even do this when you don't mean to at all, as Bourjaily *père* learned on the Big Hole.

Love,
Dad

. . .

Homestead, IA

Dear Dad,

I've enjoyed these reminiscences, too. In fact, trying to write some fish stories myself has prompted me to reread some old favorites. Looking through Ray Bergman's *Trout* the other day, I came upon a story about grayling that made me think about my own experience with the fish in a new light.

In 1933 Bergman made his first trip to fish for grayling in the Elk River in Colorado. He caught several, was not very impressed, and wrote an article for a fishing magazine in which he stated rather bluntly that grayling were nothing more than suckers and he couldn't see what all the fuss over them was about. Several fishermen wrote back to say that what he caught were whitefish, which look like grayling and in some places are even called grayling, the Elk River among them. Chastened, Bergman went on another trip, this time to Yellowstone, caught a lot of real grayling, and became a big fan of the species.

Maybe you can already see what I'm getting at, but let me quote from A. Laurence Well's *Observer's Guide to Freshwater Fishes*: the grayling is a "delightful fish which so closely resembles the whitefish, especially regarding the mouth and scales and is referred to, and justifiably so, as 'the lady of the stream' and sometimes the 'queen, or flower of the water.'" Since I know I caught both grayling and whitefish that day, and since David and Stephen had never seen either before, it seems obvious to me that they made the same mistake Ray Bergman did in confusing the two. Therefore, I caught the only grayling on the trip, and some of the tarnish is removed from my one and only fishing accomplishment, the Big Hole Grand Slam. *Living Fishes of the World* puts the average grayling at 12 to 16 inches, and mine was nothing if not average. I think he was probably closer to 12 inches than to 10, as I used to think. Put up quite a tussle, too.

My shameless revision of the grayling story (I *believe* what I just told you) and our differing memories of camp cooking in Montana and other events lead me to the following conclusion: The act of fishing only begins with the catching of a fish. Over the years we build on the original grain of truth until we've formed a pearl that may bear little relation to the event that inspired it. While the IRS may frown if you try that on your tax return, it's a harmless enough vice if confined to fishing. In fact, it's almost mandatory, since the evidence is so often eaten, released, or lost. If fishing needs any justification, we can do so by deeming it an acceptable outlet for creating the small fictions about ourselves we would like others to believe.

Good luck as you pursue the wily mahseer, and I look forward to a highly readable, if only reasonably true, account of the quest.

Love,
Philip

. . .

Bombay
On the eve of
flying home

Dear Philip:

Shortly after we got here, three months ago, I saw a stuffed mahseer in a wildlife exhibit downtown. He was about 30 inches long, shaped like an Iowa River carp, and had dime-sized scales that were badly wrinkled. He was also a faded yellow-brown and very dusty. He looked like a sluggish, unpalatable fish to me, which made my next discovery easier to shrug off.

This happened when we got to Kashmir, and I found there was to be no resolution of my doubts in the land of the Shalimar Gardens. It's been years since anyone caught a mahseer there—exactly as many years ago as the construction in Pakistan of some much-cursed systems of hydraulic-power dams, which left all the mahseer on the Pakistani side of the border.

If you hear of dams being blown up over here, it's neither military action nor terrorist saboteurs. It's fishermen.

This is not to say I did no fishing at all. I went once. Once was many more times than enough. The fish were brown trout, and the procedure is one of the least likable inheritances from the British.

There are good trout streams in Kashmir, and they are, like the ones in England, I guess, divided into beats of a mile or so each. You get a license to fish a particular beat. No other. But how was a fellow to know where the beat began and ended? Easy. The beat-keeper would be at his shoulder every step of the way. I'd have tried to tell the smiling little old guy who showed up that I really enjoyed fishing alone, but our chances of having any kind of understanding linguistically, hedonistically, or piscatorially were about what they'd be if one were to go on a saltwater fishing trip with a porpoise.

I had, for tackle, a light spinning rod. Spinning, said signs along the creek, was not permitted. So my man cut about ten feet of monofilament off the reel, tied it onto the rod tip, and we took the reel off the rod.

The stream, when we reached it, was maybe twenty feet across—big rocks, small pools, and in full flood. There was no way of presenting a fly in it, swished around from a rod tip with ten feet of monofilament. The place was totally deserted. My beat-keeper looked anxiously around, however, and then, finger to lips, tied on a small Mepps for bait. And Oh, hell, I thought, we haven't even started yet, and we're caught already, because another guy appeared suddenly, wearing some kind of turban. Did Kashmiri game wardens wear turbans?

If so, not this kind of turban, I guess, because this kind was worn by a friend of the beat-keepers, whose function, apparently, was to be my instructor. In fact what he wanted, stationing himself at my right shoulder (the beat-keeper was as close as he could get to the left one), was for me to hand over the rig. Puzzled, I let him have it, and he pointed to the pool I'd been planning to try first and flipped the little Mepps over that way for me. If he'd hooked a fish, do you suppose he'd have let me try to land it? He didn't get one, though, but I managed to get my strange equipment back from him, and in the course of the next hour or so caught three nice, pan-sized browns. The two Kashmiris never left my side, until I decided I'd had as much sport as a fellow could be expected to take and paid them off. About all I can recommend for this manner of fishing is eating the browns with some nice, fresh, hot local chutney made with mint, vinegar, chiles, and coriander leaves.

Chutney, it turns out, is not something sweet and brown

put in a bottle by a man named Major Grey. The word covers all kinds of interesting cold sauces.

End of Indian Fishing Report, except for this: Yesterday I took the kids to the Bombay Aquarium, and about the first thing I saw was a tank full of live mahseer. These were gorgeous-looking fish—bright, silver with gleaming scales, and extremely active. The biggest one was about 3 feet long and built, come to look over him, more like a linebacker than a carp. And it's said that down in southern India there are national parks where the water is not divided into beats, and one license fits all. The mahseer fishing is supposed to be splendid.

Agreed: This correspondence is fun. It was nice of David Seybold to get us started with it. Let's do some more. My next letters will probably come from Maine, where we're going for a while after we get home from India and get shaken out.

Love,

Dad

Chapter 2

———

JUDGE, HE WAS DELICIOUS

Brunswick, ME

Dear Philip,

This is a long way from my little red house in Baton Rouge, in the vicinity of which freshwater fishermen sit at anchor watching bobbers, beneath which dangle split-shot and hooks baited with crickets. When a 6-inch bream is caught, there is satisfaction, if not exhilaration. Uncatchable mullet flip exuberantly in and out of the water, and inedible gar rise to the surface to sun themselves. There are said to be good bass lurking around the cypress knees, which I don't doubt, but the exciting fishing is in the salt water of the Gulf, an hour away, for redfish, snapper, and speckled trout, and for big-game fish farther out.

Here in Maine, fresh water is something else. John Yount came by yesterday to eat a decent number of lobsters and invited me to join him and Art DeMambro on what sounds like a rather scary fishing trip for landlocked salmon. The west branch of the Penobscot, where they're going, is a river that draws more white-water nuts than fishermen. Those who wade do so cautiously. John and Art are taking a canoe, with a small motor, a big anchor, and John's considerable experience from his own white-water feats.

"Love to go," I said with my best weasel smile. "But don't worry about making room for me in the boat. I'll just fish from shore." I believe John chuckled.

We didn't talk much about the fish, of which I know nothing. Tomorrow I shall do some angling at the Bowdoin College library, though I'm aware of the ancient wisdom that says you can fill your creel with facts but you can't sauté them *amandine.*

Love,
Dad

. . .

Homestead, IA

Dear Dad,

Glad you're going on another fishing trip; you haven't done enough of that in the last few years. But why you would leave the safety of your polluted, gator- and cottonmouth-infested Louisiana bayous to go fishing with John Yount, of all people, is beyond me. Remember, it was John's white-water canoeing partners who, as Yount legend has it, waited until he was safely aboard the plane home before they fell to their knees and kissed the tarmac chorusing, "He's gone, he's gone, and we're still alive."

The last time you and I went fishing with John—and it must have been about 1971—he took us on a whirlwind tour of northeast New Hampshire during which time I fell into three of a possible four rivers in the space of three days. The biggest and whitest-watered of these was the Androscoggin, which John himself admitted was "pretty rough," although he also promised it held trout "as big as your leg." I don't recall seeing too many leg-sized trout as I bounced around the bottom, but it certainly was wet and cold down there.

Incidentally, the Androscoggin flows into the Atlantic right near Harpswell. If you get a chance you might check with the Coast Guard and see if ever they picked up any of my stuff.

Love,
Philip

. . .

Brunswick, ME

Dear Philip,

My best fishing buddies in the dark waters of the Bowdoin library were Byron Dalrymple, Derek Mills, W. B. Scott, and a man with a perfect name, Anthony Netboy. From their works the following is cheerfully plagiarized: Landlocked salmon are a non-migratory form of *Salmo salar*, the Atlantic salmon. People used to think there were two distinct kinds of landlocks—the sebago and the ouananiche—and each kind was classified as a separate subspecies of the Atlantic. Today we've pretty much decided such distinctions were over subtle; all Atlantic salmon, migratory or no, are now tossed into the same taxonomic pot.

Exactly how landlocks get landlocked is open to question. Some may have been trapped in fresh water when their river systems were rearranged by glaciation. Others, however, have a clear shot at the sea but don't take it. The closest that men ever came to establishing Atlantic salmon in the Pacific was at Lake Te Anau in New Zealand. The fish crossed them up. They had access to the ocean, but chose freshwater life and were doing fine until the introduction of brown and rainbow trout; the salmon are very scarce now.

In Lake Ontario, which, in 1835, had an enormous population of landlocks, they aren't just scarce, they're extinct. On the Canadian side it's claimed that someone once landed a 44-pounder. Our North American landlocks, living principally in Maine and eastern Canada, have analogues in Sweden, Norway, Yugoslavia, and Russia. If you happen to be fishing in Sweden, just ask the folks around Lake Vänern what's the hot fly for *blanklax.*

Lake Sebago, Maine, is where the unofficial U.S. record fish was caught, back in 1907. It went 22 pounds 8 ounces, and I'm not at all sure I want one anywhere near that size on my line two weeks from now, dragging John's canoe toward the rapids. That name "ouananiche," by the way, is an Indian word meaning "he drowns you in the water and laughs like crazy."

Sea-run Atlantic salmon are fished for on their spawning run, when they aren't feeding, and no one understands why they take flies at all. But landlocks are easier to catch because they feed year-round; my authors say they readily take flies, spinning lures, and various trolled baits, probably including live goats. When they can't get goat, smelt is their favorite food—landlocked smelt, actually—so that streamer flies like the Gray Ghost are recommended.

I'm advised that the best fishing is just after ice-out and again in September, neither of which corresponds to late May. I'm also advised that landlocked salmon hunt their food in rough water, as if I needed to be reminded.

But my next fishing place will be L.L. Bean, which should be relatively safe and a lot of fun. I'm to meet Art there on the way to the river.

Love,
Dad

. . .

Homestead, IA

Dear Dad,

You think a visit to L.L. Bean is safe? Ask the next guy you see sleeping on a park bench under a pile of old Herter's catalogs. Chances are the last thing he remembers is going into Bean's tackle department to buy some leaders. Just thinking about the place makes me want to spend money I don't have. If you see anything I need, like a couple of popping bugs or a 16-foot bass boat with a chart recorder and a really big outboard, put it on my Visa.

Since you seem determined to go ahead with this trip, let me add to what you have told me everything that I know about landlocked salmon.

The main thing I've found is that they don't get nearly as much press as their more glamorous sea-run cousins. In *The Salmon*, however, J. W. Jones does devote a few paragraphs to theorizing why landlocks got landlocked. He draws on the observations of a guy named Ward, who studied the phenomenon of landlocking when a power dam in Washington created Lake Shannon and, consequently, a new population of landlocked sockeyes. The salmon tried to find a way downstream, but were turned back—not by the dam itself but by low water and warm temperatures. The fish retreated to the cold depths of the lake, where they lost the urge to migrate.

Having reported that, I realize I've done nothing to advance your practical (i.e. how-to-catch) knowledge of the landlocked salmon. All I can really do is wish you good luck.

Apprehensively,
Philip

. . .

Harpswell, ME

Dear Philip,

You were right, except Art was already waiting when I got to L.L. Bean, which is probably all that kept me off the park benches. Being observed prevents a true shopping frenzy from developing. Even so, having been away from fly fishing for ten years, I was grabbing stuff with both hands and my eyes closed—flies, fly boxes, tools, waders, shoes, and a new reel and line for my old bamboo Orvis. The rod was treated as a curious antique by the salesmen, who kept calling one another over to see it.

On the five-hour drive from Freeport to the river, I learned more from Art about our fish. They look like seafaring salmon in the development stage, called "grilse" when they come in after their first year at sea. Landlocks aren't as great a table fish, Art feels, but then he doesn't think any freshwater fish matches up with those from salt; I suspect he's never eaten walleyes. Anyway, landlocked salmon flesh is white, not pink; the minimum keeper is fourteen inches, and spinning gear is used as commonly (and legally) as the fly rod.

Got my first look at the river from the car ten miles before we reached camp. It looked reassuringly smooth. Got my second look a minute later, and it was still smooth enough, but a yellow raft full of guys in wet suits and crash helmets went tearing past at just a little less than the speed of light. The road, as well as the campsite where we found John's pop-up, is owned by a paper company. Huge trucks loaded with logs careen by from time to time as an added hazard, and there is a metal barrel on wheels near our spot with DANGER: BEAR TRAP lettered on the side.

On the camper was a note: "Am at the Holbrook, looking for supper. John." Art had his rod case out of the car while I was still reading this. I barely had time to notice that, while the place is quite primitive—no electricity or telephones—the woods are rather open. There's birch and a variety of evergreens, but not much underbrush. Holbrook is the name of one of the pools we'll be fishing. This evening Art and John ferried me 150 yards across it. The current was even stronger than I'd imagined, and the rapids above and below the pool even noisier. Each paddle stroke John took from the stern, and each one he instructed Art to make in the bow, was calculated and precise; seeing them work got rid of some of my tension.

Still, I was happy to have my feet under me while I tried to recover a fly-casting technique that was never more than five on a scale of ten; nor was I back up to three when, watching my Adams drift past on the surface, suddenly I had a fish. It was a beautiful little 10-inch brook trout, and catching it delighted me more than I'd anticipated, until I realized this was because the rest of my tension about the river was gone.

Hell, I loved this river. The constant roar of the rapids, which started twenty yards below me, was great.

The pull of the current against my new waders was invigorating. I'm ready for salmon, and ready for bed. Will write again when I get back to the coast.

Love,
Dad

. . .

Harpswell, ME

Dear Philip,

The second morning I caught a salmon. I'd walked a mile up the bank, enjoying the spray and the smell of balsam, casting now and then, till I reached a pool called the Little Eddy, which is big enough to hold a couple of kidney-shaped football fields, and very deep. There's a rock ledge that goes sixty yards up the north edge, from which I could cast and cover maybe two percent of the water, but fish were rising within range.

A small hatch was on, and I scooped up one of the fluttering creatures it consisted of, something with brown wings and a white body. Naturally, the closest I could come from my L.L. Bean collection had white wings and a brown body. I decided not to use it. John had given me a generous number of flies he'd tied for the trip, among them an Atlantic salmon fly called a Bomber. It looks like a bit of horse dung tied to a size 8 hook. "Salmon like it dry," John had said, "they don't like it wet." It was close to the wing color of the insect I'd looked at.

I kept it dry, and on the fourth cast a fish hit and dove that made my recent brook trout seem insincere. "Landlocked salmon are a strong fish," Art had told me, but I was amazed to see, from the first of many leaps, that my fish wasn't more than seven inches long. I put him back, and many more like him in the next four days.

The biggest salmon I caught came, as the books had predicted, out of the roughest water I fished. Again, it was off a rock ledge, and I was using the Bomber again, mostly because it was big enough to see when cast directly into the rapids. This fish hooked himself and ran in that fast water so strongly I was sure I'd lose him, fishing at my mentor's advice with a 2-pound test tippet on my leader.

The tackle held, and I beached my fish on the rocks. He looked enormous.

Just then Art came along with his canvas Orvis creel, which has a ruler printed on it. We measured, and I had a 15-incher, and Art a couple more like it. But at camp we compared Art's creel ruler with a metal one John keeps and found that the canvas had shrunk greatly during the years, the ruler with it; my fish was thirteen inches now.

So, in five days of fishing long hours, I didn't catch a legal landlocked salmon, but I sure did eat one. Judge, he was delicious.

John had caught four legal fish, Art two. They were disappointed, and it didn't help to notice that the guy at the next campsite had so many big salmon he was smoking the excess ones. We introduced ourselves, of course, and inquired about his method. "Well," he said, "I tie these." And the thing he held out for us to see looked more like a cigarette than a trout fly—a long, white cylinder of clipped deer hair with red stripes down each side, nothing like my now-bedraggled Gray Ghosts, but clearly far more resembling a smelt in the view of a fish.

If I can't find a Rapala or something that looks like that next time, there'll be nothing for it but to buy, well, let's see: fly-tying kit, plenty of deer hair, extra-long hooks, white lacquer, illustrated book on smelt . . . Have I survived the river only to be borne by treacherous currents into the jaws of L.L. Bean on my way back to Miami?

Love,
Dad

•   •   •

Homestead, IA

Dear Dad,

I see that I have failed utterly in trying to act as a stabilizing influence from afar. Maybe I can go with you next time. Get two of everything at Bean's just in case.

Love,
Philip

Chapter 3

DOLPHIN TIME

Miami Beach, FL

Dear Philip,

"Now that I sometimes live in Miami," I said to myself, looking out at the amazing expanse of bright blue-green water sparkling off Miami Beach, "it behooves me to wonder if there may not be a fish out there and, if so, how would a fellow that gets behooved by such matters go about catching him?"

For, in spite of the many hours of my life spent getting water in my boots in trout streams and scratches on my legs from blackberry thorns on the banks of farm ponds, I know nothing of the pains and pleasures of saltwater fishing except what I've read in the works of E. Hemingway and T. McGuane.

Is that statement 100% true? Not nearly.

Once, while I was in college in Maine, I joined some small boys fishing with nothing but shiny bare hooks and hand-lines off a bridge over a tidal river and helped them fill ten or twelve buckets with little 10-inch tinker mackerel in something less than two hours. Never saw fishing that fast in fresh water.

And a couple of times I became the illustration for the only saltwater fishing truth I know, which is: "Surfcasters do not catch striped bass, but they do get the occasional and unnerving blowfish." Not even the slimy sculpin I caught once in Elk Creek caused as much alarm as I felt the first time I unhooked a fish that inflated himself in my hand until he looked like a balloon at a surrealist kids' party.

Once I caught a 12-pound striper, but from a boat, not the beach. It was John Yount's boat, and the bass towed us all over Great Bay. We'd been fishing for sole and had some, which reminds me that a fellow I met in Lima, Peru, took me out on the bay there to try for flatfish. It was very deep where we anchored, and I absolutely could not get a feel for the difference between a bite and the current tugging with that much line out. My host, however, having done it before, kept hauling up a nice fish every eight or ten minutes. I felt pretty silly.

On the way back from South America, on a freighter anchored off Panama, one of the seamen asked me to hold his rod for him while he went to the head. He'd barely left when I felt a mighty tug. I set the hook with no idea what I was fishing for, and then watched the line run out, then stop. I cranked, knowing there was something heavy and strong out there and noticed my line was heavy and strong, too. Back came the sailor. He took the rod and horsed in a shark of some kind that I'd guess weighed about fifty pounds. Small but scary when he was flopping on the deck, showing us his teeth. I noticed our leader was a piece of chain. They killed the shark with an ax, the man who held it doing a kind of dance step to stay out of harm's way, and then threw it back in the Pacific, where I assume other sharks found it soon enough.

And once—I'm turning out to be a veteran saltwater guy after all, but still know nothing about it—I hauled in a monster of the deep. This was in Uruguay, years back, when I was fishing with Reuben, who ran the resort hotel at which we were staying and also ran a kind of fishing team, catching fish of all kinds for the hotel kitchen. The other team members were a cook and one of the groundskeepers.

We were surf casting, I have to acknowledge, and in a most athletic way, using long, heavy rods with which we took great dashes into the water to about knee-deep, where the momentum was used to inaugurate a grunting, two-handed cast to sling the bait out as far as possible. Then we'd go panting back to the beach and stick the butt in a rod holder, which is where my rod was when suddenly it bent double. I grabbed it and the others came running.

We took turns reeling in, and my first glimpse of what we had came sooner than expected and was more astonishing. What I could see were the far-spread tips of two huge, beating wings, breaking the water on either side of my line, and Reuben and the others cried both "Angel" and "Devil" in Spanish.

It was a giant ray. I can't say what kind, but its wingspread was at least ten feet. Most of it, my teammates said, was inedible, and I was all for letting the creature flap on back. But the cook had the final say, which, in this case, was that the tail was a fine ingredient in chowder, and that's where it went.

Setting aside 10-inch tinkers and 10-foot rays, I'll begin my South Florida saltwater fishing education next week, though in neither the Hemingway nor the McGuane mode to start with. My friend Virgil and I are going drift fishing on a party boat, which is pretty much tourist mode, but may be fun and a way of starting out before investing heavily for a charter. It will cost us $20 each for half a day, bait and tackle supplied, touristy beer extra, and I'll let you know how it works out.

Love,
Dad

. . .

Homestead, IA

Dear Dad,

Good luck finding fish in the ocean off Miami; as always, I can do nothing but offer inadequate advice from afar. Here's the great truth of surf casting, according to me: "The ocean is a big place." Now, I understand theoretically that there are bait fish, who feed on small things that live close to shore. Then the larger fish and birds feed on the small fish, and in turn they attract larger fish and fishermen. The fishermen, safe at the top of the food chain, can then catch these larger fish without being eaten themselves. Yes, I understand all this, but whenever I've actually stood on a beach with a surf-casting rod, heaving some sort of plug or spoon as far as I can—say, forty or fifty feet, into an ocean that goes all the way to France—I can only imagine that the odds of my lure crossing the path of a fish are infinitesimal. Nor, actually, can I ever remember catching anything while surf casting, which would seem to substantiate my theory.

I do remember catching the odd rock bass and mackerel on hand-lines in Maine and Martha's Vineyard on summer vacations. I also remember an incredible rat's nest of mono-filament I made out of another hand-line in Cozumel when I was ten or eleven, on the second of our family skin-diving trips. That was one place I was sure there were actually fish in fishing range, because I'd seen them when we snorkeled in the shallow water off the hotel beach. As you might remember, it was quite common for us to see huge schools of baitfish in very shallow water. One or two barracuda always lurked nearby, between the school and what I would presume to be the safety of deeper water. Anytime the baitfish made a tentative move away from the beach, all however-many thousands of them thinking with one collective mind, the flick of a fin or a stern look from a barracuda would send the school into a 180-degree turn in unison, their bright silver sides flickering as they caught the light. With that picture in my head as I tried to untangle my hand-line, I wondered what the chance was of any fish picking my bait over one of the millions of other things to eat already in the sea. I realize now that predators pick out the weak and unusual fish in the school—if you're a fish, conformity is good—and so my piece of whatever it was on a hook could have stood out enough to attract the attention of what? A 4-foot barracuda? Just as well the line stayed tangled after all.

Your ray, your shark, and your blowfish all remind me that saltwater fishing has an occasionally scary and mysterious side that the freshwater fishing I've done (slimy sculpins notwithstanding) generally lacks. My only rod-and-reel brush with sea monsters came on a dock on the Chesapeake Bay at that house where you left me once while you went goose hunting. Whoever was in charge of entertaining me produced a rod and some bait, and while we were failing to catch anything fishing off the dock, we noticed countless jellyfish floating past. Rerigging with one of those plastic baskets strawberries come in, we scooped up ten or eleven jellyfish, keeping one alive in a glass jar, where it undulated contentedly in the seawater until we let it go the next day. I had a hard time getting to sleep that night, knowing there was a jellyfish in a jar in the next room. At age eight, it seemed entirely plausible to me that a jellyfish could unscrew the lid, ooze across the linoleum floor, climb the bedpost, and sting me in my bed.

Since jellyfish, I assume, are not expected to make up part of your party boat's catch, this careful examination of my saltwater fishing experience shows I have no relevant advice to proffer. Presumably your skipper will. At least hope he knows how to keep the touristy beer cold.

Love,
Philip

· · ·

Miami Beach, FL

Dear Philip:

Since your last letter, I've been out on the 67-foot *Reward II* not once but twice, which must argue that I enjoyed it the first time, when Virgil was along, too. It was pleasant but desultory, so that I understood Virgil had no great compulsion to cancel a lunch date the afternoon I decided to go out again. A power lunch at the Russian Tea Room with a producer interested in optioning his novel, and featuring beluga caviar *blinis* and Stoly Bloody Marys might have been worth Virgil's missing that second trip, but not by much.

Let me set both outings for you: Miami Beach is pretty much an island, connected to Miami by a set of heavily traveled causeways. Off the southernmost of these, the Mac-Arthur Causeway, is a parklike area where you can buy flowers, take helicopter rides, board a seaplane for one of the Caribbean islands too small to have an airport, or board a party boat to go drift fishing.

We seventeen half-day-sports began arriving about nine o'clock the calm and sunny morning of the first trip in our T-shirts, baseball caps, and shorts or jeans, as touristy-looking a group as ever was unwilling to rise and fish at the crack of dawn. The proprietors of the *Reward II* and her sister boats know quite well that a 9:30 departure is more salable, and at that hour we were on our diesel-powered way, up Biscayne Bay, between the causeway and the Port of Miami docks.

It took about half an hour to reach the point upwind of the reef over which we were going to fish. We were at sea, but the buildings along Miami Beach were still distinct. A fair number of smaller, private boats were out over the reef and drifting when the mate came along, assigning rods, baiting us up with cut squid, and directing every other person to fish the bottom while the next one fished shallow. It was pretty clear that we were playing catch as catch can, with no predetermined species expected. It was also clear, from the slimness of the rods and the light-looking line on the free-spool reels, that we were fishing for the skillet, not the taxidermist.

Now the captain, having (I suppose) made his wind and current calculations and checked his depth-finder, cut the power. Everybody moved to the upstream (as in Gulf) side of the boat, and in went seventeen hooks and lines. I was fishing deep and, toward the end of the first drift, had a mild but unmistakable nibble. I struck too fast, lost contact, and had to reel in and replace my bait.

"Try the bottom," I said to Virgil, and we both went deep. It was his turn to strike too fast; we agreed we'd be patient. I got the next nibble, wasn't patient at all, and hooked a fish down there anyway. Reeled up with a nice feeling of something wriggling about that tells you it's not a glob of seaweed, and brought up a slim, agreeable-looking, big-eyed fish about fifteen inches long and maybe a pound.

The mate was there to see and I said, "What have I got?"

"Sand eel," he said.

"Worth keeping?"

"Hell, that's a sweet fish to eat," he said, and took it off the hook for me and carried it to the live box.

Virgil got the next slim, agreeable-looking sand eel. In fact, he got the next two. Then I alarmed everybody by catching something that couldn't have looked fatter or more disagreeable, a scorpion fish, with poisonous spines. The mate cut the line to get rid of him.

There was another sand eel or two on the following drifts, and a guy up forward caught a red snapper. Some of the beer got drunk, though not by us—not at eleven in the morning—and back to the dock we went. I'd say the seventeen fishermen might have had forty fish, and I was the lucky guy with three sweet-eating sand eels (Virgil had two).

No, I wasn't the lucky guy. The red snapper man was, since everyone had contributed a couple of bucks to a pool for who'd get the biggest fish, which he won. Then I was the lucky one again because he didn't want his fish, and I went home with a couple of beautiful snapper fillets along with my other sweet six.

Nice enough morning on the water and sure, I know where the Russian Tea Room is, did you say 12:30?

When I arrived at one o'clock at the *Reward II's* dock for my second drift-fishing trip, it was buzzing. There was an audible and visible energy level on and around the boat that hadn't been there at all the time before.

"The dolphin are running," the captain told me as I handed him my check, and I trust it is unnecessary to add that the word *dolphin* is used to name a beautifully colored, wedge-shaped fish, as well as a marine mammal dear to TV fans and a football team that has fans of a somewhat different kind. As for the fish *dolphin*, its fans are chefs and their patrons. I'd been seeing dolphin advertised as the daily special, prepared in various styles, on the chalkboards of fancy restaurants all over Miami.

This time, when we started drifting, everyone was told to fish shallow, and the lines were lightly weighted. The bait floated out there, fifteen or twenty feet away and five or six feet down. The first drift was unproductive. The second was frantic.

It had just begun when twenty fish appeared, swarming toward us as if summoned by sorcery, gleaming and irides-cent, as clear and colorful in that marvelously lucid water as fish in a clean aquarium.

When they appeared in that dreamlike way, we were actu-ally hushed. Then I watched one dart to my bait, take it unhesitatingly, and at the tug I woke up, as did pretty much everyone along the rail. No more hush—we were shouting now, hooking fish and reeling them in, and I was astonished to feel a hand on my shoulder. It was the mate.

"Leave him in the water, but hang on," he said and moved along.

"It's so the school will stay with us," the man next to me explained, and I was willing to play it that way for a minute or two. But there were still fish swimming fast patterns at what seemed like arm's length. I brought up that first one, an 18-incher and heavy, and trotted it back to where the mate and his kid assistant were stationed by the live well. They took my fish.

"First one?"

"Right," I said. Many of those who hadn't been asked to leave the first in the water had two by then.

"Five on the head," the mate said. "Remember it." And, dispatching the dolphin, he cut five little notches where the neck would be if fish had necks, to identify it as part of my catch. I stepped back to look for just a moment. Dolphins, while not graceful looking—the bodies taper back from a bulldog kind of head—are nevertheless beautiful because of their coloring, electric blue with shiny spots as they come out of the water, although the color soon fades.

Wow. And back in quest of more daily special went I.

Our captain knew what he was doing. He kept us among schools pretty constantly all afternoon, losing a school now and then, finding it again, or perhaps another. Sometimes there seemed to be schools of a hundred or more. Things would be calm but tense. Then I'd start seeing flashes and shadows coming up toward us that would resolve themselves into feeding fish as they swarmed up for the bait, hooking themselves as often as not—but striking was easy, the visibility was so good. And a tug, reeling in, unhooking the dolphin, and hustling back to the markers, with whom, after the first, I didn't tarry.

My first had been small. Most of the rest were a couple of feet long, probably running two to four pounds, and every one, in spite of the ease of catching them, exciting.

We took back a couple of hundred fish on the *Reward II* that afternoon, and there was a good deal of reasonably happy confusion on the dock where they were divided. For instance, as the mate called marks ("Two on the head," "Three on the tail") and came to "Five on the head," a young woman who'd been fishing with her seven- and eight-year-old son and daughter stepped up to claim it. She also said that they'd caught twelve dolphins, which caused the mate, seeing me step up behind, to roll his eyes in disbelief.

"How about you, young man?" he asked. "Seems to be a mix-up about the marks. How many did you take?"

I shrugged and said, "Seven, I believe," cutting myself down a couple. And he straightened it out somehow, using unmarked and unclaimed fish. I said I'd be back to get mine after they'd been filleted, and when I did return he presented me with a lot of fillets—enough for Virgil's freezer as well as ours.

The crew still had some to sell, and, as the mate said, "The idea's for everyone to have a good time, isn't it?"

If that was the idea, its time came on dolphin day.

> Love,
> Dad

. . .

Homestead, IA

Dear Dad,

I envy you your catch—when you live 1,000 miles from the nearest ocean, all the saltwater fish in the supermarket are confusingly described as "fresh frozen." I can never get anyone to tell me exactly what that means.

I dimly remember fresh red snapper, however, as my favorite saltwater fish during our endless family car trip through Mexico when I was five or six. Dolphin I recall with equal and much more distinct fondness from the time in college when you took me to the Double Dolphin (appropriately enough) in New York, where the management mistook us for someone else and bought us cognac and Rusty Nails after dinner. I've always suspected they thought you were Phil Rizzuto. The sand eels I'll have to take your word for. Still, this party boat stuff sounds like a trip to the fish market, but more fun.

But if, by accident of geography, you'll be doing the saltwater fishing for the two of us these days, you're going to have to come up with something a little more, I guess, *macho* than dangling squid chunks over a sandbar and arguing with women and children about who caught what fish. My image of the sport involves a small boat on the ocean, a shark or two, some blood (yours, a fish's, some third party's . . . at least it won't be mine), and a big fish. I'd do it myself, of course, but our water in Iowa is salt free and shark sightings are plenty rare.

Love,
Philip

. . .

Miami Beach, FL

Dear Philip,

The boat wasn't small, there wasn't a shark to be seen, but I've done a day-long charter on the open sea, way off soundings. The boat was the *Fantastic II* out of Key Largo, and the closest thing to a small boy in the tale is her owner and skipper, Justin Hopper. Justin is nineteen, wiry, blond, feisty, full of energy, admired by other charter guys for his fishing knowledge and instincts, and says things like: "Marlin are like speeding tickets. You get one when you least expect it."

I'm not sure what my expectations were—got neither a speeding ticket nor a marlin—but the other thing Justin had to say about the species endeared him to me. I'd asked him what he'd do with one if he hooked it, and Justin said: "I'd try to bring him alongside the boat, pat him, and let him go."

I need to start, however, with Dave Cox, a friend of Dave Wilson's, who bought Bill's Bait and Tackle Store in Key Largo six or eight months ago, quitting a good marketing job in New York with General Foods to do so. Old, retired guys who've heard the story are forever coming into the bait shop and saying: "Young man, you've done what I always dreamed of doing," though I doubt the dream included keeping the shop open twelve hours a day, seven days a week, as Dave and his wife, Joannie, do.

Dave Cox consequently does what fishing he can at night, and night was when I first got aboard the *Fantastic II*. I was with the two Daves at the shop and had just met Justin, who proposed we all go yellowtailing. That expedition was the first demonstration I had of Justin's virtuosity with baits and techniques for the great variety of ocean species. He started learning practically in the cradle, and has focused his life on both the sport and commerce of fishing.

For the yellowtails, it was commerce. Dave C. put up the bait and chum; he and Justin were to split the catch, and extra hands meant more lines in the water. As we went out in the dark, over the big coral reef that stretches intermittently all the way from Miami to Key West, Justin was watching his depth-finder and fish-finder constantly, the latter equipped with an eerily lit screen, rather like the ones on computers, on which shadowy groups of fish showed up pretty frequently. I can't tell you how he knew which were the yellowtail snappers, but once he saw them at the depth he wanted to work, Justin seemed quite certain.

We anchored, put out bags of chum, and the skipper started what he called a chum line as well, drifting many buckets full of ground-up fish carcasses off the stern until I could imagine a cloudy column of them rising from bottom to boat.

Then we baited spinning rods with cut bait, let off the bails, and allowed the bait, too, to drift unweighted, down with the chum. The yellowtails rose up to the bait as if they'd been waiting for an elevator, and we met them coming and brought them in. Beautiful fish, fast fishing.

It was workmanlike, it was fun, and it made me feel like an insider, though I quickly acknowledge that I couldn't do it on my own, even after participating, even if I had a boat, equipment, and friends. Nor could I have duplicated the obscene fisherman's insults shouted back and forth by Justin and some fellow in charge of a boat that anchored nearby, which had to do with the character of anyone poaching another guy's chum line. It sounded seriously meant to me; turned out the other skipper was a friend of Justin's and their discourse standard offshore visiting procedure.

We got back after midnight with more than a hundred pounds of fish to clean, and I learned next day that Justin and Dave C. had made $79 each. Dave W. and I each got some nice fillets from the smaller fish and yep, yellowtail is terrific.

Preparations for an all-day charter were painstaking and elaborate. We had a mate along, a good sized, black-browed veteran I'll call Fred, in addition to good-sized, redheaded Dave W. and my bald, undersized self. They couldn't throw me back, though; I was paying the bill.

When I got to the dock, Fred and Justin were unpacking and storing frozen bait. We were going to be trolling 10- or 12-inch fish called ballyhoos, which look like a cross between a small gar and a flying fish, with extended, beaklike lower jaws. Then there was tackle to rig and check, instruments to set, the engine to test and fuel up, and a number of other things I really didn't comprehend. Dave, who's worked for Justin on occasion, is pretty handy around a boat. He was making a contribution, as was I, mine being to keep nimbly out of the way.

We covered a good many miles of deep water that day, trolling those teaser-rigged ballyhoo because we hoped for marlin. If we'd wanted—or expected—tuna or sailfish, I was told, we'd have been drifting and fishing with live bait.

Once shore was out of sight, all the ocean looked pretty much the same to me, but Justin seemed to have destinations in mind out there. He stood up one flight, at the helm and the wheel, while Dave and I sat in chairs in the cockpit, and Fred stood between us, ready to give me guidance and fresh bait. In addition to Dave's rod and mine, there were ballyhoo out on the two outriggers, and from time to time one of us would go up on the bridge to stand with Justin and watch for sign.

As you suggested in one of your letters, we were looking for flocks of feeding birds, but I learned that there's other
sign out there as well. Weeds are one, and we hadn't been out
long before Justin spotted a patch, moved us over to it, and
turned to troll along the edge, which sent me back to my
chair and rod.

Baitfish like the weeds for protection, which gives them
something in common with farm-pond minnows, after all,
and the larger fish work the edges, which gives them something in common with farm-pond bass.

But nothing happens on a farm pond like what came
next—our captain shouting out "Port rigger," the mate grabbing the rod, setting the hook, and handing the rig over to
the customer so that he could land the fish. Which I, being
the customer, did without much fuss, since the fish was a
smallish barracuda that we sent back to resume grazing the
weed patch.

Another sign is slick water, and after a while Justin saw
some of that and moved us into it. Within the next four or
five minutes we caught four or five nice dolphins, of about
the same size we'd taken from the party boat. It seemed to be
a rather small, isolated school, though, so the action didn't
last long. Still, I couldn't help being impressed that, out in
this trackless expanse of waves, Justin was actually getting us
into fish.

It wasn't long after the slick that we saw birds feeding for
the first time, hundreds of them, and I got excited. They were
swirling en masse like a big whirlpool in the air, the ones in
the vortex diving and screaming. Justin got us into position
to go by the flock; up one side, down the other, and finally
right in amongst them.

Nothing happened except we kept going, leaving the
birds, which went back to feeding. I was puzzled. Fred explained.

"If we make a couple of passes and they don't take, we

figure they're bonito. You don't often catch one, and when you do, you don't much want it."

And a little later Dave hauled in a free-agent bonito—a not-bad-looking, slim, blue-and-silver fish a couple of feet long—and Fred put it in the live box calling out to Justin, "Something for your dogs."

Justin has a yardful of dogs, who apparently have no objection to middle-sized members of the tuna-mackerel tribe, unaware, I guess, that their owners are hogging the groupers, yellowtails, and real tuna.

While we were eating sandwiches and drinking pop (beer didn't sound good to me on a hot day on a lightly pitching boat), Dave caught our first respectable fish, which they said was a jack crevalle. It was a yard long, and I gathered the dogs weren't going to get this bluish-silver, yellow-finned dancer. Jacks are rarely found so far offshore. It caused a certain wonderment.

Early in the afternoon we saw birds feeding again, went to join their luncheon party, and again it seemed to be bonito kicking the baitfish up to where the birds could get them.

It isn't only big flocks of birds fishermen watch for. Certain solitaries, like the long-winged frigate bird, one of my favorites to look at, are fish sign as well. There were several we managed to get under, but none turned out to be the spotter plane we hoped for.

There were other sights worth seeing, out there off soundings—most memorably a 12-foot sea turtle, which went down slowly, unalarmed, as we passed by, like some sort of peaceable submarine.

We joined a big flock of feeding birds for the third time in the middle of the afternoon, and this time it wasn't bonito. We'd just reached the edge of the flock when rods and riggers started twitching and bending, and we found we were in a school of much larger dolphins than any I'd seen before. Dave was catching them while Justin was adjusting boat speed. Fred was about to hand me a well-bent rod from one of the riggers when I felt something hit the rod I was holding with a real jolt.

"Hit him," Fred said, putting the rigger rod back in its socket. I yanked up on my rod, and there was no question but that there was a moderately large fish hooked out there.

What followed then was, I expect, the result of the mate's being aware of my inexperience. I wanted to let that hooked fish run, try to check him, reel him in, let him run again or dance or sound, but Fred wouldn't have any such book-learned nonsense. He started bullying me, really, and, thinking myself more neophyte than client, I gave in.

"Crank it," he yelled. "Keep cranking. Don't stop."

Justin was using the motor to help me, and Dave and Fred were on either side of my chair, watching and encouraging, ready to take over if I got too arm weary, as I soon would have.

When it was close, I could see it was a dolphin again, but a dolphin five feet long, and still full of energy for the tussle since he'd been horsed in. Fred had the gaff ready, Justin called for Dave to take the helm, and I brought the big dolphin up to the transom. Fred snatched the fish out of the water, and, to my astonishment, Justin leapt down from the bridge and swarmed all over that fish like a middle linebacker making sure of a tackle, wrestling it all over the cockpit, getting himself joyfully messed up with blood and slime.

It may not have been an equal contest, but it was a splendid sight.

When we had the fish subdued and the hook out, Justin and Fred lifted it together into the live box; it wasn't all that heavy, actually, but it was still pretty active. When we weighed it later, it was forty-two pounds, very close to what Justin and Fred had estimated. So we had our considerable fish and it was time to head home.

Fred said, as we went: "There are plenty of guys who specialize in dolphin fishing who've never got one like yours.

The record's eighty-seven pounds, but yours is as big as any I ever saw."

Conclusion: I had a nice time on the water, learned some interesting stuff, but didn't feel like I'd gone fishing. Justin decided where to take the boat, Fred handled the bait and the rigging, the fish hooked itself, and I followed Fred's insistent instructions to crank it in, whereupon Fred boated it. You could train a monkey to do my part, but this is not to demean deep-sea fishing.

Rather it's to say I came to it too late, knowing too little about a complex sport; even if I had my own boat and a good mate, I'd still be in other people's hands as to what to do.

I might go again sometime, though it's expensive, in the hope of seeing a billfish—marlin, sailfish, or sword—though I never was a trophy hunter and don't feel I want a big fish on any of my walls, either. It might be hard, at that, not to keep a swordfish for eating, and Dave tells me marlin are pretty good edibles, too. And I wouldn't mind getting into a fishing situation again like the night of the yellowtails, where each man is making his own decisions, at least at hooking and landing time.

Anyway, I'm sure there's more to learn, even another totally different kind of saltwater fishing, but if I get into some more I'll save it for another set of letters.

For now, my only regret is that I can't send you some of the beautiful 2- and 3-pound dolphin fillets I've got in the freezer "Fresh frozen," which I guess means frozen before they spoil. You should hardly ever buy the other kind.

Love,

Dad

P.S. Dave Wilson made a number of corrections in the fore-going, so perhaps we can grant him this postscript. Quoting now from his letter:

> Please note that at the time I told you marlin are good
> to eat I should have explained further. What I should have

said was, "When I was in Bimini the locals told me that in the old days they would grind the marlin flesh and make it into a kind of marlin burger." I got the impression that they still do, today, but that they don't admit it. Today the marlin is considered the king of game fish, and any civilized man who eats one is considered corrupt . . .

When Justin told us that catching a marlin was like getting a speeding ticket, he didn't tell us that in all the years he's been speeding around the Keys he's only had one ticket, though he regularly pushes one hundred per and never uses a radar detector. He's caught about the same number of marlin. . . .

Chapter 4

MOVING ON TO SHARKS

Dear Philip,

This will begin a second series of communiqués about my belated, old-geezer education in saltwater fishing, in which, as we begin, I have earned a grade of D (for Dolphin) in the first series. I think I'm about to raise it to a D-plus, before I move on, as I will, to fishing of kinds other than trolling dead bait in the deep blue sea.

This we have done, and will once more, in the hope of catching a variety of fish, with a several-hundred-pound marlin, a creature so far unseen by me, as the great prize.

At the end of piece one, I was somewhat doleful about my role as a troller. With more tutelage from Dave Wilson I've come to understand what goes on out there a little better.

Deep-sea fishing turns out, after all, to be a team sport. Dave had got us invited to go out with Doug Warfield, a man retired from the retail oil business, who has a nice, 30-foot Samas—a boat from a line much favored in the Keys, built by a Greek family. Doug likes to drive it. Now, if you think driver, rigger, and fisherman instead of captain, mate, and

51

customer, you have started to formulate the team concept. Add the thought that we are now fishing as sportsmen, amateurs, rather than as clients of professionals, and perhaps the team notion grows clearer. What may also grow clearer is that it would be extraordinarily awkward, if not impossible, for one sportsman to fish for big game by himself—and not much fun, unless you like things arduous, for two—three is the proper number, as is nine in baseball, two in honeymoon bridge, and a thousand in *pulu*, as played by Persians on horseback a couple of millennia ago. There is some question in my encyclopedia as to why they reached over for the Tibetan word for *ball* to name their game, but the Persians have always indulged in far-out things.

Well, then, as Dave said to me as we started out and he began expertly to rig six poles—two from the stern, two from the edge of the bridge, and two on outriggers, with ballyhoo as long as your average brook trout for bait—"You're the fisherman. Your job is to watch all the lines, grab the pole when we get a strike, and land the fish."

It was a rough day, alternately exhilarating and wretched, trying to stay balanced, but away we went, over the reef and into the deep water. We came to an undulating line of floating seaweed that stretched away as far as I could see and that indicated the edge of the Gulf Stream. It wasn't long before the starboard outrigger popped off its clip, and I did grab the pole and give a heave to set the hook. Doug cut the speed to idling. I could feel a good, heavy fish out there and deep. Then there came a lot of slack in the line, and Dave called, "He's turned toward the boat," but Doug had already seen that and started us forward fast. Pretty soon I had the slack taken up and could feel the weight of the fish again, and was starting to move him in when the line really went slack, and I said, still cranking, "I think he got off." It proved to be the case, and I asked my teammates what I'd done wrong.

"Nothing," they said. "You don't land every fish you hook. Having one get off happens all the time."

It was their guess from the speed with which he'd come after the boat and the depth at which he came—for he never broke water—that it might have been a wahoo. They are an extremely speedy fish, by all accounts, for which special fishing tournaments are held. At the time, Dave was hoping to fish in a wahoo tournament off the Bahamas, so I guess we hoped it had been a wahoo, since the thought that we might have hooked one raised the possibility that there'd be others.

By then Dave was rerigging, Doug was following seaweed, and I was watching lines again. But when we hooked and landed another fish, it turned out to be a dolphin. Although not nearly the size of the one I'd caught with Justin, he was powerful enough at twenty-odd pounds so that my arms got really tired bringing him in through the strong sea, in spite of the help Doug could give me by maneuvering.

I don't think, candidly, that I'd have the strength to land something really big by myself, like a marlin or a sizable tuna, and I said as much to Doug and Dave. They assured me that when I learned to reel in properly—which is what the fisherman on the team must learn to do, of course—it would come easier.

It's a matter of rhythm, rocking forward with the rod, during which movement you get a little slack and crank, and then straightening up to firm the line. But even when, from time to time, I'd get the rhythm, I realized that a fight with a large ocean-going fish really can be a physical contest, for which I continue to doubt I'd have the endurance to win.

We'd been talking, between strikes, about sailfish, which apparently run fifty or sixty pounds, generally. I'd been learning that, off the Keys where we were, the method is to drift live bait, motor on and idling, boat pointed into the wind. (Off northern Florida, in what's called Sailfish Alley, they troll for sailfish just as we'd been doing in the hope of marlin.)

"But," Dave said, "sailfish are show fish, not fighting fish. Sailfish are wimps." Note: It costs a couple of thousand bucks to have one mounted.

Hey, sailfish, don't tell Wilson, but I think I'm one, too.

Love,
Dad

. . .

Homestead, IA

Dear Dad,

Although I always preferred team sports to the individual kind when it comes to games where you win or lose (the ones involving balls, oars, or, if we're going to play "can you top this obscure game" here, goat carcasses, in the case of the Afghan game of *buzkashi,* which is probably related to *pulu* in some way), hunting and fishing are different. Some folks think the more people you can get together to go hunting or fishing, the more fun you'll have. Me, I always thought the fewer people in the group, the more fun you have. With deep-sea fishing though, I can see how even just showing up requires more than one person.

So, mulling around this fishing team idea, the key seems to me to be picking the right position to play. Clearly "rigger" is not the man to be, nor "fisherman," who, from your description, pays a lot of money just to do heavy lifting. "Captain," however, has a nice ring to it. Driving the boat includes, in my understanding, a good deal of the actual playing of the fish, as well as the making of all critical decisions, as demonstrated so ably by Justin Hopper and Doug Warfield.

I bet it's kind of fun to play fish from behind the wheel of a 30-foot Samas. I have driven for anglers before, of course, except they were dangling plastic worms for bass and I was trying to keep the bow of the rowboat pointed in the right direction. I know it takes a sure touch to guide the boat in deft counterpoint to a fish's every move, although I do it with less finesse than most. Said Pam, on the occasion of her catching her first fish (a nice bass of some three pounds) while I worked the oars and shouted advice, "Stop splashing like an idiot so I can land this fish."

So, do you suppose you could charter a boat and have the captain do the reeling while you drive? Surely they must carry collision and liability on those things.

Okay, probably not. Next idea: What about bonefish? They have them there, don't they, on the Gulf side, along with permit and snook? All these, my tackle catalogs tell me, require flies not much different from the deer-hair bugs I like to throw at bass. And I know that a monkey cannot be trained to fly cast, although I guess if you sat him at a typewriter long enough, he would eventually write a book about it.

> Love,
> Philip

· · ·

> Miami Beach, FL

Dear Philip,

If Huck Finn were the author of this report, his freckles would be fluorescent.

Well, this here's explorer fishing, Tom, 'cause you ain't sure what you're a-going to see— Oh, all right, I'll stop it with the prose, but I do guarantee that you ain't sure.

You might, for example, see one of the rare, surviving saltwater crocodiles—that's right. A *croc*, not a dumb old gator like you see all the time. I haven't, so far, but there's a big refuge for crocodiles out in the back country, which is a stretch of water a hundred miles long, starting from the Everglades and going up the Gulf side of the Keys, from Largo to West.

The backcountry's got hundreds of uninhabited keys in it, and there can be fish along the banks of any one of them. There can be birds to see in the sky overhead such as bald eagles, not to mention your everyday falcons, ibis, roseate spoonbills, and those wonderful formations of shorebirds in which every individual seems able to turn and wheel at the exact instant all the others do.

What you don't see is other people and other boats. You have the illusory feeling of being the first human to glide along the edge of this Key or mangrove swamp.

I've been out four or five times now, with Cox and often Wilson. Cox has poled the boat, a craft that can move in water teacup deep when poled; it can also come close to flying across the big expanse between Key clusters, at the cost of some pretty good hats that otherwise need to be held on the head with both hands, or, more simply, sat on.

Arriving at a likely looking bank the first time out, I watched Cap'n Cox climb into a four- or five-foot tower and start to pole us, and thus participated in my first episode of sight fishing. The tower man spots a fish and gives you coordinates—like, "Between those scraggly mangroves and that stupid stake. Might be a redfish."

Then you cast, probably using a live shrimp, though sometimes it's an artificial not unlike the ones we use for freshwater bass. Flies, as in your catalogs, seem to be pretty much for the bonefisherman—and the bonefish, you'll be surprised to learn as I was, live not in the backcountry but on the ocean side, over shallow sand flats. (Tried over there a couple of times, once wading and once by boat, and saw exactly as many bonefish as I have saltwater crocs.)

The desirable backcountry fish are, as you suggest, snook and permit, plus tarpon for excitement, along with speckled trout and redfish. It wasn't, by the way, a redfish at all that D. Cox saw the first time out, nor did he say it was—what we saw, that day, was a ray and some sharks. Sharks love the backcountry. Wilson told me about seeing a kind of shark dormitory, where several hundred were sleeping, side by side.

We caught nothing the first time out. Second time, or maybe third, I did hook a shark, a black-tip about two and a half feet long, estimated at maybe eight pounds, and said to be fine eating. D. Cox saw a pair of them, and, when we got within twenty-five feet of them, so did I. Cast them an artificial and watched them bat it back and forth like some kind of underwater ping-pong ball. They had a kind of kid's-stuffed-animal cuteness—appealing big brown eyes and nice, well-shaped, pouty lips. When I got the one who took the bait over to the boat—he wasn't much of a scrapper—Cap'n Cox said to release him. Too small. I guess by the time you get one butchered and cut crosswise into steak, there isn't much meat there.

Only one of our several trips was productive, though there was always interesting stuff to see. On the productive, or quasiproductive trip, Wilson was spotting and poling while Cox and I fished. What D. Wilson spotted was moving water along the bank of a certain key. Tidal current. And the moment we reached it and I tossed in a shrimp, I had a fierce bite, a small but stubborn fish trying to make it into the mangrove roots where a line can be snagged and a fish can get loose. This one didn't, and shortly I had him flopping on the deck, a two-pound, useless, saltwater catfish. Next up, smaller but as good a skirmisher, a jack crevalle. Do we keep him? The two Davids laughed as one. And another catfish—Cox pulling up and discarding stuff, too—and something called a ladyfish. Keep her? More laughter.

A fish hooked and missed.

> Cox: "Set your hook, Vance."
> Catfish number three.
> Me: "When do I get something to keep?"
> Wilson: "You've got to pay your dues."
> Cox, a paid-up fellow: "My God. Oh my God,
>   this is huge."

He was indeed into something considerable, hauled it away from the mangroves, and we were off on a sleigh ride. It was something four to five feet long, and heavy. A giant snook, we yelled. A record redfish. A bottom-running tarpon. A CROCODILE AT LAST.

Then he was close, and we saw him. Shark. Species undetermined as he finished biting through the leader and disappeared.

Huck would have had Pap's shotgun and finished him off.

Love,
Dad

. . .

Homestead, IA

Dear Dad,

I've neither fished the backcountry nor finished reading *Huck Finn*, so I find myself without literary or sporting context in which to frame a reply, which has not been unusual during the course of this one-sided fishing correspondence. I am glad to hear, however, that there remain several square miles of Florida without retirement communities as yet built upon them.

My failure to finish *Huck Finn*, incidentally, is a matter of record. In grade school we took a test on the book, including the following question slyly designed to determine whether we'd finished reading it: "In the last chapter, Huck and Jim's escape is nearly ruined by a friendly big dog who follows them down to the river—True or False?" Thought I, marking *F* on the paper with my pencil, who would use anything as tired as the old big-dog-down-to-the-river trick in a classic like *Huck Finn*? Mark Twain, apparently. *F* again, this time in red ink.

Having skipped ahead to the end of your last letter and checked carefully, I find that there are few big dogs in the backcountry, but apparently there is more than a little bit of everything else—some of it to catch, most of it just to look at. So, on the basis of your reports, I'll say that the backcountry sounds absolutely fascinating and is therefore the place for me when it comes to saltwater fishing. Backcountry fishing, since it's done by sight, appears to be the fishing equivalent of one of my favorite things to do as a child on vacation, which was to take glass-bottomed-boat rides.

There was one glass-bottomed-boat trip, put on by our hotel in Cozumel, which did feature fishing, although not by me and not with rods and reels. One day while you were off poking around in Mayan ruins in the jungle, Mom and I went along with fifteen or twenty other guests at our hotel on a tour of the local coral reef, during which four of the hotel's busboys jumped over the side with spear guns and shot lunch, which was then fried to perfection by the hotel chef on a remote beach. I remember being surprised that the busboys brought in an inedible-looking and spiny but actually quite delicious cowfish as part of their mixed bag from the reef.

Here, as always, I find myself again veering onto the topic of food. To wrench my thoughts away from fried cowfish and back to the question at hand: I believe you can have your sailfish and dolphins and marlin and the ocean and the beach. What I want to do now is get out on the backcountry and see a shark dormitory, a saltwater croc, and, with luck, the elusive big dog of the Keys.

Love,
Philip

. . .

Miami Beach, FL

Dear Philip,

On reflection, backcountry fishing, while appealing to the boy in me that still likes to poke around, takes a lot of time in proportion to fish caught and is pretty expensive. Sort of thing a guy would like to do now and then if he had his own boat. Still, it's really appropriate for those who, like boys and genuinely retired geezers, have a real taste for leisure. I don't yet. I want to get out and get into it, and get on to the next thing—which may be possible farther out in the Keys where there are, reputedly, lots of bonefish, even on the Gulf side. Or in the Bahamas, where the guides advertise themselves with names like Bonefish Bill, Bonefish Bertie, Bonefish Ben.

Is there a Bonefish Beatrice and can I be her Dante?

Well, I can reach a saltwater conclusion for now, which is not very consistent with a lifetime prejudice in favor of fly-fishing small streams for trout. In fact, it's quite the opposite and pretty lazy.

Though I'll go Hem or Huck from time to time, if the situation's favorable (no more six- to eight-foot waves, thanks anyway, and let's take turns cranking), this thing turns on what sort of boat I'd buy if I were to move to the Keys. It wouldn't be a 30-footer, and it wouldn't be a shallow draft affair for poling. It would be a nice, relaxing, 18-footer—no bridge, no towers, no outriggers—just a pleasant boat with dependable, not notoriously fast motors, like the one in which Dave Cox's father was nice enough to take me out. You lose no hats in a boat like that. You don't go out unless it's calm, either, and you go no farther than the reef—fifteen minutes, maybe twenty. There you anchor, chum, fish deep or shallow. The nice, sunny day I'm recalling, we fished deep. Got me some grouper strikes—no groupers—but three fine, unusually large gray (same as mangrove) snappers. Excellent supper. Nice time. Worth mentioning, but nothing to talk extensively about. Suited me fine.

Love,
Dad

P.S. This time the postscript is mine, not Dave Wilson's, though old Wilson was there for the fun. We were in the boat of Dave's friend Lee, a saltwater fly-fisherman who carries fly rods that would reach across the average street from tip to grip. The fun was sharks. Dozens of them, maybe over a hundred.

The place was the backcountry, but not much more than a couple of hundred yards of it, two football fields, side by side. When it started, we'd been getting into some smallish trash fish. I hooked a jack that seemed like it might go ten pounds or so and was reeling this guy in prior to releasing him when his weight increased ten times, then went down to zero. A 4-foot lemon shark had grabbed my fish and lure and had made off with quite a bit of line before it broke.

So we followed what seemed to be his line of departure. The water was shallow enough so that we could watch him go at first, and within a minute or two he led us into the area where the sharks were resting. Mostly there were pairs and singles of black-tips, spaced out at 10-foot intervals, but there was one fascinating pair of bonnet-heads, which are like small hammerheads, but with the corners of the hammer rounded. There was a pretty big nurse shark that came by, arousing not much interest, and in fact none of the resting sharks seemed interested in us, either. We cast. They slumbered. Then Lee made a cast with his improbable fly rod to another lemon shark, this one a six-footer. The fly landed right in front of him, and Lee said, "He can't see straight in front. I've got to get it to one side."

So Lee landed the next cast pretty much in the lemon shark's left eye. The shark took hard and went tearing off with as much line and backing as Lee had on the reel. Just before it ran out, Lee checked and broke off the fish to save his rig.

Then we more or less stopped fishing and boated around, looking. Sharks. Four kinds. All sizes. That was one of the good days that makes a guy look forward to going out again.

Chapter 5

HOW TO
END A SECTION

Hyderabad, India

Dear Philip:

It was clear from the moment we decided to continue this correspondence to book length how this section would have to end.

I would have to return to India, catch a mahseer somehow, and write you a climactic report of the feat. I would include the heart-stopping first rush of the mahseer when hooked, the strength and delicacy required to reel him in through his element of current and rock (for the fish is very adept at snagging and breaking line), and, finally, how I landed him without injury, then the weighing, releasing, and celebrating.

Failing this, concluding this correspondence might have to parallel the advice Lester Young is supposed to have given Miles Davis when Davis, criticized for playing chorus after chorus on his solos, said: "The thing is, I never know how to end a song."

"Try taking the horn away from your mouth," Young said.

So I came back to India, this time with two rods—my light one and a 7-foot, one-piece, heavy one Dave Cox built for me, the kind Florida boys use for tarpon. The reel for the big rod has 200 yards of 20-pound test on it, and along with these and a tackle box full of things like large Rapalas was a great big, awkward rod case, extended to accommodate the 7-footer. It would have held three or four more quite easily and it got me some mighty quizzical looks as I took it through airports and customs desks.

I'd done my homework this time, much of it through close reading of an 1874 classic called *The Rod in India* by Henry Sullivan Thomas, Madras Civil Service (Retired). He'd caught every kind of fish on the subcontinent, including mahseer in the 90-pound range. And from some more current articles and pamphlets I'd learned that there were still a few places that held the King of the River, and that the best might be a stretch of twelve well-patrolled kilometers along the Cauvery River, between Bangalore and Mysore, in the south Indian state of Karnataka, and controlled by that state's tourist bureau at the Cauvery Fishing Camp.

That's where I was headed; my father-in-law, the old police inspector, had made reservations for us for December 15. We would fly from Hyderabad, where I was booked to give lectures on the 13th and 14th, and then on to Bangalore.

On the 12th, as we got ready to leave Bombay, rioting broke out in Bangalore. There were sixteen people killed, hundreds injured, roads blockaded, the airport closed. It looked like cancellation time, but three days later the situation was reported calm in Bangalore, though it wasn't more than a day after we left Hyderabad that rioting started in that city. As things opened up ahead of us, they closed down behind us. I should add that violence is so common in India today—you learn from each morning's paper where it occurred yesterday—that it's taken in a pretty matter-of-fact way.

In Bangalore we found that the booking office, Jungle Lodges and Resorts, had us down for the Kabini River Lodge; the Cauvery Fishing Camp wouldn't open for another month they said.

Now the Kabini River Lodge looked pretty appealing. So did Goldie Hawn, who'd stayed there recently and whose photograph in the gardens there was very much in the center of pictures on the wall. She was on her way to see wild elephants and maybe a tiger, if she got lucky, and her hair really did look gold. That's what one did at the Kabini, watched big animals; it was once a local maharaja's hunting lodge. I was tempted. Then I took another look at that albatross of a 7-foot rod case, and listened to the Inspector, who'd been coping with the vagaries of travel in India for a good many of his seventy-seven years.

He figured if we went on to the camp, they'd fix us up one way or another. We engaged a car and driver—make that antique taxi and cabbie—got directions, and off we went. It was a rather slow sixty-five kilometers, the last fifteen or so of which, after you go through a village called Bhimesari (where the chief crop is mulberry bushes, from which leaves are gathered to feed silkworms), is a series of brief, bump-to-bump flights.

The camp, however, was a pleasant surprise. We'd been told there might not be any tents in service because of damage from a recent flood, but there were actually two, one occupied by an Englishman, who'd caught and released a small mahseer—a 3-pounder—that same morning. While the Inspector, who loves travel but doesn't fish, checked the second tent and visited the kitchen, for which we'd bought supplies, I walked across the mud to the riverbank.

The Cauvery, which is sometimes called the Ganges of the South, is big. It looked at least a quarter of a mile wide, with a good strong current and plenty of rocks. But then, when I got to the edge of the water, I saw that our luck, which had held pretty well so far, had run out.

"If you see the river discolored," says *The Rod in India*, "you had much better not waste your labor. . . . Wait til you can see with ease the small pebbles at the bottom in four feet of water. . . ."

I could barely see a big rock on the bottom in two feet of water. The river hadn't finished going down since the flood we'd been told about.

Nevertheless, I went back to the tent and uncased the rods, and as I did, both the guide and his assistant (called a "gillie" in my old English book) showed up, decided I should start fishing with my smaller rod, and inspected the contents of my tackle box, with its forty or fifty bucks' worth of brand-new plugs and spoons.

"No Mepps?" they said and shook their heads sadly. The big, expensive Rapalas, which Cox, Wilson, and I had thought would be the winning ticket, were scorned. They finally allowed that a small Rapala might do and that they could permit me to try a gold spoon as well. Then the guide took the rod, the gillie the tackle box and landing net, and I followed them down to the river, where a particular stone was pointed out, downstream of which I was to make my first cast.

I'm happy to say that I managed to get my lure to the spot, not that it produced anything. I was, as a matter of fact, somewhat less upset by this close attendance than I had been a couple of years back when the helpers showed up at the trout stream in Kashmir, about which I wrote you.

These fellows were full-time professionals who knew the river and knew the fish. I was willing to learn, and after a bit the guide decided that I was competent enough at this kind of fishing so that he could go off, and he did, leaving me with the gillie—who now took over indicating where I should place each cast. Figuring he was practicing up to be a full-fledged guide himself someday, I told myself, "When in Karnataka, do as the British did," and we got along all right. We weren't getting any strikes, though.

The sun was going to set over the other bank of the Cauvery, where we might see wild elephants bathing in the morning, just like Goldie. The gillie and I turned back, and went to a spot near camp that had seemed likely to me—

plenty of rocks and a comfortable place to stand, under the wide branches of three big banyan trees. It was there that I was reminded that fishing in India often becomes a spectator sport. First the guide came back, this time with a friend, to see how we were doing. Then the Inspector showed up; he'd made a friend, too. Our driver came back next, followed by two small boys. And then a thin old man in a loincloth and frayed white shirt, with white beard-stubble on his face.

Then I was aware of movement around and behind them, looked back and saw an unbelievably scrawny child, sitting on its haunches. Looked again, and saw it was a rhesus monkey with a pinkish-brown face. No, it wasn't; it was the scout or leader of a troop of fifty rhesus monkeys with pinkish-brown faces, who followed the leader quietly, single file, to one of the banyan trees, which, one by one, they climbed. They were about the size and maybe a third the weight of a Border collie, with long tails, long arms, and a look of total, unruffled composure.

I didn't start fishing again until the last of them had disappeared up into the banyan leaves and boughs. Then I went back to casting into the sunset, retrieving from the now-darkening water. I don't know what made me look back again, but when I did, my ground-floor gallery had been joined by an audience in the mezzanine. Some of the fifty monkeys had distributed themselves along the lower branches of the banyan trees and were keeping track of every cast I made.

Dusk fell, and we went off to supper and to sleep, to dream of 90-pound mahseer and 3-ton elephants.

Of course, I dreamed of no such things. I was in this taxi in New York, naked from the waist down so that I didn't want to get out, trying to get the driver to let me call my dog, Marigold ("I told you, she'll sit on the floor").... Never mind. In the morning I was up early enough to make a few casts with the big rod, unobserved. There were no elephants bathing across the river—same dumb flood that clouded the water scattered the elephants by giving them bathing pools in the forest. Then the gillie and the guide caught me. Tea was ready, they said, and so was the special bait. I knew what that was going to be and had hoped to avoid it: doughballs.

When in Karnataka, don't do as the British did a hundred years ago after all; do as one particular Englishman, now departed, did yesterday, when he caught his three-pounder. The water was still cloudy; none of my lures had attracted any attention yesterday. I enjoyed the tea and gave in to the doughballs.

So we fished what they called the mango pool because it does have a big mango tree spreading out over much of it. The doughballs, which are a far pleasanter substance than the stinkbait doughballs for catfish back home, are used the same way. The stuff is formed around a treble hook, cast in, and allowed to sit at the bottom, where current gradually dissolves it and the fish smell it and follow the trail to the hook.

It worked okay, too; it was me who didn't. I started getting bites right away, light ones, then heavier; tried to set the hook and came up empty. Went through this about four times, and on the fifth finally did have something on, fair-sized but no heart-stopping rush. I reeled it in without much fuss and was congratulated on landing a pink carp of eleven or twelve pounds, which would make a great lunch, my instructors said. Then the guide illustrated what I must do to hook a mahseer—apparently a very hard-mouthed customer—by starting with the rod tip just about touching the ground and whipping it up as fast as he could, all the way over his shoulder.

Then I caught another fish, a smaller, common carp this time, which we put back.

And then not me, but our driver, who was playing with the small rod while I worked the big one, hooked a mahseer, not that we knew what it was at hooking time.

The guy handed me the rod, I reeled in, and again there was no particular struggle—but then what could one expect from a little fish one foot long and less than a pound?

"Silver mahseer," cried the gillie. "Do you want to take a photo?"

"Baby mahseer," I said. "No, not this time."

But I'll say this: My mahseer (or was it the driver's?) had big, bold, bright scales, and the flesh of its mouth, unlike that of the pink carp, whose lips looked like they'd been injected with milk, was firm and clear. The eyes were large and sparkly; he was shaped long and trim, maybe a little like a barracuda, but without visible teeth (the teeth are in the throat). He'd be a fighter someday, even a King of the River, but for now he wasn't even a prince. Call him a princeling; let him go.

. . .

Master of the anticlimax, I had, on a doughball, with a rod handed me by a Bangalore cabbie who'd set the hook, landed and released an extremely small mahseer.

At least there weren't any monkeys watching.

Love,
Dad

PART TWO

C'MON, DAD

My earliest memory of my father's hunting is seeing him in our kitchen, just returned from a day in the marsh. He was wet and muddy, still in rubber boots and canvas coat, showing me four or five equally wet and muddy snipe. They didn't even look like birds to me, then, just small brown blobs with long bills. While I was growing up, Dad hardly ever came home warm or dry from the field. Hunting, I inferred, was often uncomfortable and sometimes a little dangerous.

I don't ever remember my father mowing the lawn, fixing the roof, or cleaning out the downspouts. Instead, I watched while he threw himself into outdoor projects: making decoys (both wire geese and injection-molded ducks); digging post-holes for a quail flight pen; building a tree house for deer hunting; blasting potholes with dynamite; building and stocking ponds on our farm; planting trees and shrubs for wildlife; cleaning out wood-duck boxes; reloading shotgun shells; tying flies; training dogs. I remember, too, that he was often gone, hunting quail in Mississippi, ducks in Saskatchewan, grouse in Wisconsin, geese in Illinois, even jaguars, once, in Mexico. From my four- or five-year-old's perspective I recognized all these activities as a form of play, but as an intense, adult type of play quite different from what I did with my friends.

When I was old enough to keep up with the hunters and dogs in the field, I went along on pheasant hunts, carrying a Daisy Red Ryder. Once I could carry the BB gun safely in the field, Dad told me, I could move up to a .410 and real shells. When that time finally did come, I said, having never given the matter a moment's thought until then, No, I don't want to kill anything, and stopped joining my father in the field.

Dad has always insisted—in what I think to be an extremely noble bit of parenting—that my refusal to hunt didn't matter to him and he was proud of me for making up my own mind. I don't know. As a recent father myself, I can guess how hard it must have been for him to accept my feelings about hunting as stoically as he did.

I can understand now, too, how the enthusiasm of the next generation of hunters sustains the enthusiasm of their fathers in the field. While he still hasn't admitted it, I think Dad's passion for hunting waned in part because I didn't want to go with him. By the time I did start hunting, as a senior in college, Dad didn't hunt much at all anymore, except for the occasional foray close to home for pheasants or rabbit.

In his introduction, Dad said he's interested in the reasons why I finally started hunting. I've thought hard about why I hunt, and I really can't explain it other than to say I finally tried it and liked it. I can't come up with anything more to say than that when I finally shot my own dinner, it seemed perfectly natural.

What I can describe in more detail is when and how I started hunting. I was, as I said, a senior in college and home for a bit of an extended Christmas Break in 1979. Dad suggested I join him on one of his hunts—armed walks around the farm is what they really were—and I agreed, because there really isn't much else to do in rural Iowa when the temperature hits 10 on a good day and all your friends have gone back to school.

We had two shotguns, both 12-gauges: a Browning Light 12 Auto-5 and a Beretta ASEL. The A-5 had a righthanded safety, so Dad took that for himself and handed me the Beretta, whose tang safety was suitable for both right- and lefthanded shooters.

The Beretta was an over and under, a medium-high-grade gun sold by Abercrombie & Fitch under its own brand name. My mother bought the gun for Dad in 1963 for the then enormous sum of $500 after she had come into a small inheritance. At the same time she bought herself an expensive saddle and me about 4,000 Lego blocks.

The Beretta has a straight-hand stock carved out of a dark, elaborately figured piece of walnut, checkered at, I'll guess, about twenty-four lines to the inch. The forearm is very slim for an over and under, so it was made of quite plain, straight-grained wood for added strength. Floral scrollwork covers the coin-steel receiver. The barrels are twenty-eight inches, originally choked modified and full, designed with cornfield pheasants and decoying ducks in mind. Lightweight by American standards, the Beretta made a good quail, grouse, and woodcock gun, too, when Dad could find brush loads for it.

That first day, however, the Beretta did nothing but carry nicely and look good—the birds ran ahead and flushed wild, blown quickly out of range by the cold north wind. But the chase was exciting, and I was delighted to have a reason to be outside in such miserable weather.

By the end of the afternoon, red-cheeked, chapped-lipped, and exhilarated, I had decided, to my great surprise, that I loved this pheasant hunting.

The next day we went again. This time I flushed a cock pheasant in range, and missed him with both barrels.

Dad seemed as caught up in the excitement of the hunt as I

was, and he announced, when we came in, that if we were
going to hunt pheasants, we would do it right. After dinner
he called Vern Zach, an old family friend who'd once run
cattle with my parents and had since switched to raising
field-trial champion German shorthaired pointers.

The dogs found more than enough birds, and I missed
several, but finally, as the sun sat low on the horizon, angling
golden light across golden stubble, the dogs bumped a
rooster, who crossed thirty-five yards in front of me, right to
left. That shot gives me trouble today, and it was much more
difficult than the straightaways at pointed birds I'd already
missed that day. This time, though, when I slapped the
trigger, the rooster cartwheeled hard into the cornstalks. I
felt excitement, sadness, and deep satisfaction all at once. My
father clapped me on the shoulder, and Vern took the pheasant from the dog Peter Gunn's mouth and handed it to me.
From that moment on I haven't really wanted to do much else
besides hunt.

I'd like to say that that day made Dad a hunter again, too,
that his passion for hunting was rekindled the moment mine
was ignited, but it wouldn't be true. I do think a few sparks
were struck, though.

Dad had begun teaching at the University of Arizona
every fall semester, and he left his gun with me in Iowa each
August when he left for Tucson. I hunted doves with it in
Illinois a time or two and pheasants and ducks around home,
all with spectacular ineptitude. Once I jumped a flock of
thirty wigeons off a puddle in a cornfield. They rose so close
to my feet that I had time to miss twice, open the gun, fumble
for two shells, reload, and miss twice more. In my early
twenties I was learning for myself the lessons I should have
learned ten years earlier.

And, while Dad hadn't returned to hunting right away, my
newfound enthusiasm proved gradually contagious. I took
him into the field more often when he was back in Iowa, and

in Arizona his students Dave Wilson and John Brenner did the same, hunting quail and doves in the desert.

I'd taught myself to hunt deer, and one fall I assumed the coaching role usually taken by the senior member of father-son duos, guiding Dad to his first and only deer. (You'll read about it in this book's chapter called "Venison"). By that time he was hunting quite a bit once again, and it seemed like a good idea to send him his old gun. I did, along with the antlers of his buck (a spike) that I'd had mounted for him.

This past year, though, Dad sent the gun back to me again. He has bursitis in his shoulders, and it bothers him to the point where he can't shoot a 12-gauge without quite a bit of pain. So he switched to a 20-gauge—a $125 pawn-shop autoloader with a Polychoke—and left me his gun a second time.

Dad had used the Beretta hard over the years, from Saskatchewan to Mexico, and he'd abused it sometimes, too. I can remember watching him use the forearm and barrels to scrunch down the top strand of a barbed-wire fence before he swung his leg over. Deaf in one ear from too much shooting, he was oblivious to my shouts of "Hey, cut it out. That's an heirloom!" After twenty-five years of that kind of treatment, there wasn't much gun left. That's not just my opinion, either: thieves broke into Dad's car in a motel parking lot one night shortly before he sent me the gun. They took some Karmel Korn, a few towels, a road map of the southeastern states, but left the Beretta behind.

When I put the gun together, I realized those thieves might have been smarter than I had originally thought. I could see where the Karmel Korn would be easier to carry and probably worth a little more, too. When I wiggled the gun by its grip, the action rattled like a pair of dice. The ejectors had grown narcoleptic with age. The rib was smashed flat against the top barrel at one point, where I suspect Dad might have used it as a pry bar. The bluing was worn off in some places, spotted with rust in others, generally faded to the color of a mackerel that's been lying in ice at the fish counter for a few days. The grip was deeply cracked, the gold-initialed medallion missing, the forearm nearly in pieces, the checkering a mere memory. Deep gouges marred the stock, and most of the oil finish was gone. Even in that condition, it was a nicer gun than any I'd ever be able to afford. The coin-steel receiver still gleamed, the gun pointed and swung beautifully, and I could remember that first rooster crossing in front of me whenever I looked down the mangled rib.

Last winter I sent the gun to the Orvis gunshop in Manchester, Vermont, and asked gunsmith Pete Johnson for his diagnosis. "I work on a lot of Berettas," he told me on the phone, "We have fifty in the shop right now. I've never seen one as worn out as this."

"Is the gun safe to shoot?" I asked, seeking some kind of bottom line.

"Safe is a funny word," he said. "You might shoot it for years and not have any problem. I'll put it this way: I wouldn't do it myself. I make my living with my hands."

Well, I thought, so do I, sort of. I mean, I could type with my nose, but how would I get paper into the printer?

I gave Dr. Johnson the go-ahead to perform the gunsmithing equivalent of reconstructive surgery on every last square-inch of the gun, plus some open-heart on the innards. I had him bore out the chokes to improved cylinder and modify and lengthen the stock with a recoil pad while he was at it, all for much more money than I care to think about right now.

I debated at length whose initials should go on the medallion: Dad's VNB, since that was the original inscription, my PMB, or Chipper's CGB since, if all goes according to plan, the gun will be his someday. I thought about leaving the medallion blank, too; a good gun should outlast several owners. It occurred to me, on a strictly mercenary note, that the gun might be easier to resell if the new owner could put his own initials on the stock.

Finally, I chose my own monogram. The Beretta isn't a museum piece to display or an heirloom to preserve for the next generation or an investment, nor is it for sale. It's a bird gun, a good one, and the good ones deserve to be used. I've finally got it back now, just in time for the fall hunting season. The work Pete Johnson did is simply amazing—he's stripped years off the gun's apparent age with a file, sandpaper, and elbow grease.

I won't let its pristine good looks deter me from taking it into the field every chance I get, for pheasants, grouse, quail, woodcock, and who-knows-what other birds over the next thirty-five years or so. Someday I hope Chipper will want it, and I'll try to pass the gun along to him in better shape than it was in when I got it. But who knows what lumps lie in the gun's future, and thirty-five years from now the Orvis gunsmiths may have to put it back together all over again.

Meanwhile, Dad's turning seventy makes me finally think of him as beginning to get old. I can remember ten years ago, when he and I were hunting pheasants with Vern Zach and a friend of his, and the three of us noticed that Dad had disappeared. We shouted to let him know where we were, but he didn't answer.

"Your dad doesn't have heart trouble does he?" Vern's friend asked anxiously after Dad had been missing for five or ten minutes. The man was somewhere in his sixties himself, heavy, red-faced, carrying a battered Winchester Model 97 he'd probably bought new in 1940. His expression told me he'd reached the age where he and his friends were having heart attacks. I was first taken aback by his question, then I started to worry myself. The thought of my father's health failing had never really occurred to me before: in those days Dad beat me rather routinely at tennis. After ten minutes Dad emerged from the brush. He was fine. With his deaf ear and his earplugs in, he'd lost track of the rest of us and couldn't hear us calling.

Now we're both ten years older, and while at thirty-four I may have lost half a step and most of my hair in that time, the gulf between sixty and seventy seems much wider to me than does the one between mid-twenties and mid-thirties. But Dad tells me that he feels great, that he's heading into his seventies without any major ailments and still plays tennis with his students several times a week. I only have to look at my landlord to see that seventy isn't necessarily old. Seth Eimen, the retired farmer who owns the house we rent, turned eighty-one this year. As I write this, sitting in front of an air conditioner that's working full blast, Seth is outside in the hot sun, up on a tall, shaky ladder painting the trim on the second-story windows. Last summer he built us a deck. He and I have hunted deer together every year I've known him. He first took up turkey hunting at age sixty-seven, and there's no apparent end in sight.

Even so, I have a nagging feeling each time Dad and I get together for one of our infrequent hunts or fishing trips that it may be the last time, so I commit each one very carefully to memory. Last winter I visited Dad in Baton Rouge. Friends of his had arranged a snipe hunt for us, although I decided to leave my gun at home and maybe take a few pictures instead. Our hosts dropped us off in a wet pasture, the sort of cover that snipe adore.

The grass was short and the birds were skittish, and most of them flushed well out of range. One, however, waited a little too long before streaking off low over the ground. As it banked up high and to the left, Dad made a long shot, and the snipe fell dead on its back in a large puddle. At the edge of the puddle he handed me his gun and took one step toward the dead bird, then disappeared completely under the surface of the water. He told me later his feet never even touched bottom. After a moment's floundering, Dad grabbed the bird and pulled himself out of the hole, soaked to the skin. I snapped a picture of him, wet and muddy, holding up the wet, muddy snipe for the camera.

Some things, I'm happy to say, never change.

. . .

A person who appears here without introduction is my first cousin Shaun, whose father, Paul, is Dad's younger brother by, I think, one year.

Shaun is nine years older than I am, a union carpenter, a crafty woodsman and excellent field shot. He's one of those outdoorsmen you would dismiss as lucky if his luck weren't so consistent. If there is a big fish to be caught, a sack of mushrooms to be found, or a trophy buck to be bagged, Shaun is there, in the right place at the right time, year after year. Under no circumstances should you play games with him that involve money.

Shaun also owns a fine pair of pointing dogs, Alex (a shorthair) and Buck (a drahthaar), who are as good-natured, close-working, and stolid as my dog Sam is high-strung, fast, and stylish.

Tom Culp is the younger brother of my longtime friend Matt Culp. By night, Tom is a police officer; by day, he is an easygoing, pleasant companion in the field. Tom doesn't shoot all that many birds, but at the end of the day his game bag is always full to bursting because he diligently stops to pick up every last scrap of litter he finds in the field.

I met Pam at the University of Virginia in Charlottesville. Although originally from suburban New Jersey, she had no trouble adapting to a diet of deer, pheasant, and woodcock. Pam is a great cook, and many of the recipes I mention are really hers, unless they involve deep-fat frying in lots of grease, in which case they're mine. She shows some aptitude with a shotgun and enjoys shooting the occasional clay target, but Pam has a strong dislike for heat, bugs, cold, mud, and early mornings, so she does not hunt.

Chipper (Charles actually, after his grandfather and uncle) is our three-year-old son.

Pete Neal and John Brenner, like many of my father's hunting partners, were once his students. Pete I knew when I was much younger. He was a frequent dinner guest at our house and often brought a particular kind of chocolate sauce with nuts in it when he came, for which I remember him fondly. John I met only once, during the duck hunt in Arkansas. His hospitality, and his family's, was exceptional.

Chapter 6

TURKEY SEASON

Homestead, IA

Dear Dad,

For all I know you are having late spring in Louisiana by now, but here in the upper Midwest it's still winter. In years past, my major sporting activity from late February until the end of March has been the mindless acquisition of fishing tackle in an attempt to change winter to spring through sheer volume of spending. This year, however, to the detriment of the rod-and-reel industry's first-quarter profits, I found a new pastime. In February I sent twenty dollars to the Iowa Department of Natural Resources and they sent me a license to hunt wild turkeys from April 13 to April 16. Having never even seen a wild turkey before, I am trying to learn all I can in the next month about how to hunt them. I've picked up a rough idea of what to do, but turkey hunting remains a very abstract concept to me, and Opening Day will be here before I know it. I don't ever remember your mentioning turkeys before, nor have I ever had reason to ask. I'm asking now, and it's clutch time: What advice can you give me about turkey hunting?

Love,
Philip

. . .

Baton Rouge, LA

Dear Philip,

The news that you have a turkey license finds me totally without advice of any kind, thus earning us a big red zero in the fundamental father-son hunting transaction.

I do, of course, have a fussy word or two as to how you must dress and arm yourself for the hunt: a broad-brimmed, conical hat, flowing white collar, blouse, cape, and knee breeches, and a blunderbuss, with the end of the barrel flared to resemble a trumpet bell, seem correct. As to pedivesture, floppy boots with turned-down tops and square brass buckles are a must; I feel sure L.L. Bean still has them in stock.

That said, let me report that the only turkeys I ever saw were the wrong kind, or the right kind if you live in Yucatan. They were ocellated turkeys (*Agriocharis ocellata*), somewhat different from the eastern wild turkeys (*Meleagris gallopavo silvestris*) you'll be stalking.

Latin names are wonderful. The one for your bird would translate *guineafowl chickenpeacock of the forest*, whereas mine, if we agree with the taxonomists who put it in a separate genus, is *wild gift of the gods with eye-spot markings*, and I did indeed see some once.

It happened during what was supposed to be a big-game hunt for jaguars, when Harold Hughes was governor of Iowa. I was invited both as a friend of the governor's and assigned to cover the hunt for the then-endangered, now extinct, *Saturday Evening Post*. And the first thing to say about that expedition was that no individual jaguar was remotely endangered, let alone extinguished, by our presence in the rain forest.

One morning though, when I'd slept outside of camp, under a canopy of mahogany and chicle trees, I awoke to an unbelievable clamor of bird noise—shrieks, clatters, yelps, crows, and maybe gobbles—certainly nothing that could be called song. I couldn't have said how many different kinds of large jungle birds were greeting the dawn out there with me. Possibly there were guans, *currasows*, toucans, and turkeys, but the only ones I recognized were *chachalacas*, which are about the size of crows but produce more decibels than noisy little dogs.

I'd seen *chachalacas* but wanted another look and went rather carelessly down a lane, through the underbrush, which consisted of tree-sized rubber plants and philodendrons, of which I'd seen small examples in living rooms back home. It didn't occur to me to walk quietly because of the racket that was going on. Consequently, looking down the lane as far as I could, I passed within twenty yards of a small flock of ocellated wild gifts, which, more alert than I, took off and disappeared over the tops of some 16-foot-tall houseplants before I remembered the thing dangling in my right hand was a shotgun. But what birds they are: smaller than the ones you'll be after. The bare skin that covers the head is deep blue with orange decorations, and the tail spreads out with markings like a peacock's. Beautiful birds, there and gone.

From an eating standpoint, I can add that, since some of our guides on the expedition were a little faster at recollecting the shotgun than I, ocellated turkeys make wonderful sandwiches, barbecued Mayan-style and sliced thin. The only bird I managed to contribute to the table on the trip was a *currasow* that happened to be crossing the road in front of a pick-up truck I was riding in. The driver stopped, I hopped out, and the *currasow*, which is a glossy black bird, almost goose-sized, with a white stomach and a crest that curls forward, looked me over. It seemed to occur to him that he'd better do some flying away; he took a kick or two at the dust, adjusted his stubby wings, and started flapping. Meanwhile I looked up "correct load for *currasow*" in my notes, found it cross-referenced with "horned guan," checked that, changed shells, asked the driver if this really were a game bird, and found my shooting stance. By then the *currasow* was about eight feet up and hovering. A true sportsman would have reached up and caught him by hand, but me, after deliberating this approach, during which he may have got up to ten feet, I shot the *currasow*. He made a pretty good Mayan barbecue, too.

To get back to ocellated turkeys, they are and always have been exceedingly wary (so I read) and quick to fly, instead of trying to run like your *sylvestres*. The Mayans trapped them but never managed to domesticate them. Yours, on the other hand, were such easy marks that they just about put themselves away, alongside the passenger pigeon, as of course you know. By 1949, it was thought that the end of the species was just a matter of time. The story of what happened next is wonderful, familiar enough, and attributable to federal money raised by the Pittman-Robertson tax we all paid and pay on sporting arms and ammunition; I remember stopping for gas at a filling station in Alabama sometime on a spring day in the sixties and learning to my absolute astonishment that the man at the pump was planning to get him a turkey next morning. Ten years later there was a season in Iowa, and by now there's turkey hunting (so again, I read) in every state but Alaska.

Can it be so? Is pineapple to the Hawaiian wild turkey what cranberries are to the birds of New England? Can the Oahu gobbler be called in springtime with sensuous music on a steel guitar? Spring seems to be when turkeys are hunted because it's breeding season and the males can be called, but the same could be said of quail and pheasant. Except that it's because it's breeding season that we don't spring hunt. Hmmm?

Love,
Dad

. . .

Homestead, IA

Dear Dad,

Oddly, nothing I've read so far backs up your endorsement of square-buckled boots as the best footgear for turkey hunting. In fact, one of the few things I know for certain about the coming season is that I *will* be wearing hip boots. This is on the advice of a DNR wildlife biologist who has suggested that I hunt a semiflooded timber along the Iowa River bottom. He thinks I won't see too many other turkey hunters down there because most people prefer to keep their feet dry. Apparently turkeys could care less how wet their feet get, so long as no one is slogging along after them. He even told me: "You can always tell the turkeys that come out of the river bottom. They're the ones with webbed toes." I think he's kidding, but I'm not really sure.

I've also learned that we are allowed to hunt turkeys in the spring for the same reason that we can hunt deer during their November rut: Just like bucks, tom turkeys fight and establish territories in the spring. One dominant male then gobbles and displays to attract hens and does most of the breeding in that particular area. Should that turkey wind up in somebody's roaster, there are any number of other gobblers who never liked him much in the first place, ready to step in and take over as head turkey.

Turkey calling, therefore, becomes a question of making sounds like an eager hen. According to what I've been reading lately, it can be a complex business. The problem is not so much in imitating the sounds of the hen exactly, but in judicious application of avian psychology. It goes like this: ordinarily a gobbler expects a hen to come find him, and they generally do. So, if you call too much, and sound too willing, the turkey will wait, or "hang up" as we turkey hunters apparently say, expecting you to come to him. If you don't call enough, he won't pay attention. If you call too much while he is coming in you may frighten him away, although sometimes reluctant birds can be coaxed in with soft purring noises. Only a great deal of calling will induce a turkey to fly across a creek to find you.

This is perplexing stuff for a novice still trying to get comfortable with the idea of making "love yelps" with a little piece of latex stuck to the roof of his mouth. For reassurance, I called my source of commonsense turkey-hunting advice, Jesse Suber of Tallahassee, Florida. He clarified the situation admirably. "Man," he said, "if you're in the right place at the right time, it doesn't matter what you sound like. You won't be able to keep that turkey away with a baseball bat." So, maybe there's hope for me yet.

Love,
Philip

. . .

Baton Rouge, LA

Dear Philip,

As you take practice swings with your baseball bat, let me expound, not on the restoration of the wild turkey, but on the reasons for its decline and near fall. All the writers I've read seem to agree that it didn't threaten to come about because of field-clearing or forest fires. It was plain, damn overshooting, and now let me quote and summarize, from an 1878 report, the following fascinating and appalling passages. The hunters were Civil War (Union) generals, the turkey was already scarce except in Indian territory, and here is how the high officers and sporting gentlemen reduced their share of birds one night.

The author is General William E. Strong, and his title for the report, which was written in longhand as a Christmas present for the leader, is *A Trip to Indian Territory with Lt. Genl. P. H. Sheridan.* Yep. That's really Philip Henry Sheridan, who seems to have been the George Patton of the Civil War. "Stocky Phil" Sheridan's Christmas gift reached print in 1960, at the University of Oklahoma Press, with an introduction by Fred P. Schonwald, to whom I am indebted for the nickname just mentioned and everything else quoted in this paragraph and the next. "Sheridan was a stocky little man, and like Napoleon, was a martinet. He was not popular with the men who served under him and was hated and feared by the Indians."

General Strong, our author, "was probably associated with Sheridan in the West Virginia campaign." There were three other generals in the party, of whom George Crook is the most celebrated, and there was Lt. Colonel Frederick Dent Grant, the President's son, of whom "it is said that Custer incurred the undying wrath of Grant, Sr. by placing his son under arrest during the [Black Hills] expedition." Finally, the chief guide, Ben Clark, "was probably the greatest of the trackers and scouts to work for the United States Army among the Cheyennes on the plains."

Eight years after this *Canadian River Hunt*, to cite Mr. Schonwald's subtitle for the book, Stocky Phil was made a full general and given the high command of the U.S. Army; here is how he proceeded against the wild turkeys one February night in part of what is now Kansas:

> Members of the party had gone off in pairs to scout. General Strong and Ben Clark had ridden hard, seen no turkeys and got back half an hour behind the dinner hour. . . .
>
> As I dismounted, General Sheridan said: "Hurry up Strong and eat your dinner! I have discovered an immense Turkey Roost, and I will give you rare sport tonight. We must be off in half an hour!"

After a hard ride, they saw a "bold but irregular bluff, fifty or seventy-five feet in height . . . and stretching away for two miles or more, was a heavy forest of cottonwoods. 'We will find them in there,' said the General, pointing towards . . .

where the trees seemed to be of unusual height and very thick . . . in line with the highest point of the great bluff . . . behind which the sun was just sinking." The orderlies led the horses into a thicket and the hunters waited for darkness. They set out on foot, "and the light of the new moon was not sufficiently strong to prevent our frequently stumbling over down timber, or running into grape vines. . . ." So much for visibility. Nevertheless:

> "There!" said the Sergeant, "look there! That's a turkey." I cast my eye in the direction indicated. . . . On the highest limb of a tall cottonwood I saw the dark outline of an object, but I could not have said with certainty that it was a wild turkey, or even a living thing.

Mark that. Visibility again. However, the object took wing, crossed an open space, got shot, and a "bouncing great gobbler came crashing through the branches, striking the ground within four feet of where I stood . . . the forest was fairly alive with fluttering wings. It was deafening—startling—overpowering! It unsteadied one's nerves—it took away one's breath . . . in volume and intensity, I have never heard anything like it . . . I have never had 'buck fever' . . . in the days of muzzleloading guns I never fired away my loading rod, nor have I never yet put powder on top of the shot, but on this occasion, with a fluttering, struggling turkey at my feet *which I could not see* . . . in charging my gun again I dropped a shell."

The bird that he couldn't see (my italics above and below) was four feet away.

Of turkeys in their roost:

> I would estimate there were thousands . . . the air was filled with them. At every discharge they came fluttering to the trees, above and about us, alighting in many instances, on limbs directly over our heads, *not fifty feet away.* The firing began in earnest immediately after my first shot, and grew into a cannonade such as I never heard before or since on a

hunting field. General Sheridan, [Sergeant] McCann, and myself each had breech loading shotguns, and Ben Clark had a Winchester rifle. . . .

General Sheridan had had an experience of many years in turkey shooting at night, and told me I would find it extremely difficult to kill them with certainty unless the moon was very bright.

You'll recall that it was not. In spite of his 10-gauge gun, loaded with five drams of powder and an ounce and a third of number-one shot, General Strong fired six times at one particular turkey, sitting still forty yards away, and failed to drop it, much to his chagrin. He had between 75 and 100 shells with him. The moon went down. Still, he could make out the birds well enough so that he expected to kill at least 60 and predicted a joint bag of something like 180 birds for the party. He had a moment of delicacy.

> It seemed, for a moment, quite cruel and unsportsmanlike to shoot the poor birds from the lower limbs of small growth cottonwoods—the shooter standing right under them . . . they were so very near, you know; and then it occurred to me it would be better to walk back twenty-five or thirty yards, and give the birds a chance. . . . I then remembered, that it was regarded, among honorable sportsmen, as perfectly legitimate to shoot turkeys while sitting at night . . . I hesitated no longer.

He started shooting in earnest and felt that he was unaccountably missing. "Occasionally I killed or wounded a bird, but not one in four which I shot *came to the ground*." The possibility that some of the birds might be carrying shot that would later poison them didn't occur to General Strong. His gun barrel became so hot he had to get out his handkerchief and fold it into a pad for his left hand.

> It became so dark that only the practiced eye of Clark or the Sergeant could detect the turkeys . . . [but] we contin-

ued to shoot at them . . . until our ammunition was ex-
hausted. Had there been sufficient light or had our supply
of shells held out, we might have continued firing until
morning, as the turkeys would not leave the roost . . . we
had killed and *brought to bag* nineteen fine turkeys. . . . I
judge as many more were brought down from the trees
badly wounded or killed outright, but which we failed to
find, owing to the darkness. . . .

It was grand sport . . . the struggles of the wounded
birds and sharp exciting chase after the wing-broke
ones—over down timber—through dense thickets—
sometimes up to one's knees in mud and water . . . and
after all to have the wounded birds escape—as they in-
variably did when they were wing-broken. . . .

The turkeys were tied in bunches of two and three and
suspended from limbs, ten or twelve feet from the ground,
beyond the reach of wolves. . . .

By my calculation, for I expect there were a good many
more than three birds lost for every one bagged, since the
general doesn't seem to count the wing-broken nor to acknowledge that not every bird hit necessarily fell, there must
have been something like a hundred and fifty birds left
behind. The wolves had a pretty nice Thanksgiving that
February.

On another day General Strong had open shots, at sixty-
five yards, at turkeys crossing a clearing in single file and
thought he'd killed a wagonload. But only the few that fell
when he hit them were bagged. All the wounded birds that
made it into cover disappeared.

Altogether the party brought in seventy-nine turkeys,
most of them in the first six days of hunting. How many more
were killed and lost? I don't know. General Sheridan himself
ruled that only birds that reached camp could be considered
in the total bag. Body count. Part of the military mind then as
now. The boys also played euchre just about every night—
Generals Sheridan and Crook won 230 games, against 229

for Generals Whipple and Strong. A close battle, but Stocky Phil and his partner eked it out.

Write me a turkey-hunting letter to make me forget this one.

Love,
Dad

. . .

Homestead, IA

Dear Dad,

Your letter prompts me to think again about something I've wondered about before. Would I have behaved any differently from the turkey-hunting generals if I had made the trip to Indian Territory in 1878? With the benefit of hindsight, I imagine myself calling in and shooting one turkey on the first day of the hunt. After that I would have spent the balance of my stay in Indian Territory sketching the natives, or classifying previously unknown prairie plants and animals, or maybe just hanging around camp, drinking bourbon with the muleskinners and stacking the euchre deck. But I doubt it. General Strong's account, no matter how appalling it sounds to you and me today, suggests that he tried to adhere to the sporting ethics of his time, just as we try to follow the ethics of ours.

On the subject of ethics, turkeys are quite properly shot on the ground, preferably while they are standing still; shooting a turkey on the wing is considered risky and unsporting. This total reversal of normal bird-hunting protocol stems from the fact that you need to center a very tight pattern of small shot precisely on a turkey's head and neck in hopes of hitting the brain or a vertabra. No other shot will kill the bird reliably. As a result, shotguns designed for turkey hunting are unlike shotguns for anything else: they have extra-tight chokes, short barrels, magnum chambers, and, frequently, sights to help you center that tight swarm of pellets on the bird's head and neck. It's about as close to rifle shooting as shotgunning ever gets.

Not having the wherewithal to run out and buy a new turkey gun, I've instead made a cardboard cutout of a turkey head and have shot my bird guns at it at various ranges, looking for a gun and load that will kill a turkey at a reasonable distance. After much shooting and counting of pellet holes, I've settled on the Browning Double Auto and short magnum fives as the combination that most reliably perforates my target at thirty-five yards.

With Opening Day twelve days away, I am making some progress in my self-education as a turkey hunter. My calling is, well, I don't know how it will sound to a turkey, but it is getting closer to the noises on the instructional tape I bought.

I also scouted my hunting area yesterday morning. I've been out to the river bottom a couple of times during the day, to learn my way around, but the best time to locate turkeys is in the first hour of daylight, when they are gobbling on the roost.

Consequently, like duck hunters, turkey hunters get up very early. Unlike duck hunters, they leap joyously out of bed on the sunny bluebird days that drive the waterfowler to bury his head in his pillow, groaning. Turkeys gobble more on nice days, and when the alarm went off at 3:45, the sky was clear and starry. An orange glow brightened the eastern horizon; a burst gas line at the Mid-America Pipeline Company has been burning out of control for a week, twenty miles east of here.

I had to walk a mile or so in the dark after parking the truck as close as I could to the river. I stumbled through woodlots, down abandoned farm lanes, and across wide oat fields. Then I waded a shallow slough and pushed through a thick stand of willows that gave way to hardwoods near the river. I'd seen plenty of tracks down here before, but as of yesterday morning I'd still never seen a turkey.

A faint breeze from the north carried the cloying, pulpy, industrial smell of the ADM corn-sweetener plant in Cedar

Rapids. The odor, along with the sound of the river flowing past and the early hour on a spring morning, reminded me of dawn rowing warm-ups on the Schuylkill River in Philadelphia. I was briefly nostalgic but slightly irritated to have such an urban recollection after hiking a mile from the nearest road. Then the turkeys started to gobble.

The gobbling of the wild turkey is usually rendered something like "Gil-obble-obble-obble" in print, which does it no more justice than Gary Cooper's terrible imitation in *Sergeant York.* Having now heard the real thing, I can tell you there were no turkey hunters in the Academy of Motion Pictures back then or they never would have given Cooper the Oscar. What it really sounds like is if someone hooked up a pair of battery leads to a turkey's toes while he was gargling with gravel. About how I felt, too, hearing that first gobble.

Hurrying toward the sound I walked right under a roosted turkey, who lurched out of the upper branches and flew away into the morning gloom. Had it not been for the large black-and-white–barred primary feather that floated down to me in the turkey's wake, I might not have believed I'd seen a bird that large actually fly. The gobbling continued for another hour, during which I tried to locate some of the roosting trees without spooking any more turkeys.

There were at least three, and maybe five, turkeys sounding off yesterday morning. I'm beginning to think I might actually get a crack at one.

I'd wondered if I could get excited about spring hunting rather than fall. You know how exciting this spring hunting is? If I were eight years old and I found out there was another holiday just like Christmas, except that it came in April, and we'd never celebrated it before, that's how excited I am right now.

Love,
Philip

. . .

Baton Rouge, LA

Dear Philip,

I'm catching your excitement. I imagine I feel something like a basketball coach, with the game tied, the last time-out just ended, and his best free-throw man about to shoot. If you don't get a turkey, my contract may not be renewed.

Love,
Dad

. . .

Homestead, IA

Dear Dad,

You probably gathered from my incoherent whooping over the phone that I shot a turkey this morning. Now that I have called everyone I know with the news, I am calm enough to consider this turkey with an eye toward his future as an early Thanksgiving dinner. He is lying on the kitchen table as I write this, feet and head sticking out over either end. The prospect of dressing a 21½-pound bird is daunting, to say the least, and I'd like to admire him with his feathers on a little longer anyway, so I'll take this chance to give you a clearer account of my turkey season.

The MAPCO fire was flickering on the horizon like an early sunrise Tuesday morning as I drove up to the river bottom, switching radio stations, trying unsuccessfully to find a weather forecast calling for anything other than rain. I walked back to my hunting area under gathering clouds and found a place to listen. Two or three turkeys gobbled once each around daybreak, difficult to pinpoint in the rising wind. I waited, hoping they would sound off again, but it had begun to drizzle and I heard no more gobbling. So I snuck off in the direction I thought was right and sat down with my back to a large tree, hoping I was close, but not too close, to a roosted tom (75 to 200 yards is what the outdoor magazines say). A couple of minutes later, to my utter dismay, a previously invisible turkey flew down out of its roost not twenty yards away, said *"Putt!"* disdainfully, and ran off before I could identify it as a hen or a tom. Now what? Would the sound have alerted the other turkeys? How soon would they forget about me? Should I move to a new spot? When in doubt, stay put; I knew there were turkeys in the area. I stayed put and called with decreasing conviction for the next three and a half hours, hearing nothing in reply but the ever-louder patter of raindrops on my hat and the constant chattering of my teeth.

The temperature never got higher than 45 degrees Tuesday morning, it poured rain, and my slicker leaked in many places. I can't recall a wetter or more miserable morning outdoors than Tuesday's, unless it was yesterday morning. Rain fell steadily and forty-mile-an-hour gusts shook loose large branches, which fell to the ground in the dark with a crash-thump that sounded far too much like a heavy branch falling on a soggy turkey hunter for my peace of mind. I heard three faint, windblown gobbles from somewhere across the river and nothing else all morning as I sat in the mud, clucking forlornly. When a commuter jet from the Cedar Rapids airport flew low over the river, I was seized with the irrational desire to trade places with one of the dry, flannel-suited businessmen overhead, relax with a cup of thin (but hot) airline coffee, and read some annual reports.

I stuck it out for as long as I could, then went home chilled to the bone and thoroughly dispirited. I ate half a bag of Oreos for lunch and watched the noon weather report, which predicted rain for the rest of the week. It was, therefore, with extremely guarded optimism that I peered out of the window at a partly cloudy sky when I woke up this morning.

At 4:45, when I was pulling on my hip boots in the parking area by the river bottom, the sky was lightening to the color of mother-of-pearl and the wind had died down completely. I found my way to the river bottom once again and sat down next to a narrow slough to listen. Daylight was slow in coming, but the woods were alive this morning; the weather had broken. Bluejays squawked, cardinals sang, squirrels skittered up and down tree trunks. A pair of wood ducks splashed into the water just a few yards from where I sat. At 6:00 A.M. the gobbling started. I heard at least three turkeys, sounding off the way I'd heard them on my morning scouting trip. The turkey to my right sounded closest, and I knew he had the river to his back, increasing the chances he would come my way after he flew down from the roost. I sneaked as close as I dared to the sound and sat down about eighty yards from the roost tree. After waiting quietly for a few minutes I slipped the caller into my mouth and made my version of the "tree cluck," hoping I would sound sleepy but seductive. What I said was *"Puck, puck . . . puck?"* Silence. I held my breath, afraid that I'd spooked the tom. A minute passed, then another, then I heard a thunderous gobble from the trees in front of me.

Fifteen minutes later I tried another set of clucks and told myself not to call again until the turkey flew down to the ground. He gobbled back a reply, and ten minutes after that I saw a movement in the lower branches of an oak tree. The turkey leaned forward, stuck out his wings to break the fall, and flew down from the roost like a sack of potatoes with feet. Before I could decide whether to call again, he came toward me, neither strutting nor gobbling, but slinking low to the ground. Fifty yards away he stopped behind a bush and peered over the top, looking for the hen. Nothing could possibly blend in better with the river bottom than my mud-covered hunting clothes, so I stared back at him confidently through the eyeholes of my mesh head-net.

For someone who almost falls out of the tree stand every time a deer walks by, I was strangely calm as I sat motionless and watched the turkey come in. I waited until he stepped behind a tree trunk, then shouldered the gun and flicked off the safety. As the gobbler passed the brush pile I had picked as my thirty-five-yard marker, I held just under his beak and fired.

The turkey went down, wings beating furiously, and my composure evaporated completely. I ran toward him in a panic, afraid he might be only momentarily stunned. Ten steps from the bird I remembered the gun held another shell, so I skidded to a halt, drew a bead on the flopping head and missed, blowing a big hole in the mud. Then I tossed the gun aside, lunged forward, and grabbed him by the leg, forgetting that turkeys have spurs. These particular spurs were almost an inch long, but fortunately rounded and dull, so I was spared a nasty gash. What did happen was that all the flapping the turkey was doing twisted his leg around and around in the glove, wrapping the spurred leg up so tightly in the cotton glove that I couldn't let go of him if I'd wanted to. All I could do was hold him at arm's length, where I wouldn't take a beating from the big wings, and hope he was fatally hit. After some anxious moments the wing beats slowed and finally stopped. It had all been nervous reflex; several pellets had struck the head and neck, killing the turkey instantly.

After the turkey stopped twitching, I untangled him from my glove, carried him over to a slough, and washed the mud off his head. Then I took the tag from my pocket and fixed it to his leg.

Honestly, at the time I felt little more than a sort of stupefied amazement. The clear, more familiar emotions of triumph and sadness that accompany a successful hunt came later, after I'd had a chance to realize what had happened. For a while I just sat next to the turkey in the mud and stared at him. Then I hoisted him over my shoulder by the legs and began the long walk back to the truck, the turkey's thin shins digging hard into my shoulder as the heavy bird dangled down my back.

I drove to Fin and Feather in Iowa City, where the bird was weighed and I was photographed holding him. Few enough people kill turkeys around here that I was a minor celebrity this morning. I basked in that glow for a while, then came home and started calling people. And that, after two months of studying, planning, practicing, and daydreaming, was turkey season.

I can tell you this about turkey hunting as I contemplate four and a half feet of bird on the table: one turkey seems like the right number to shoot. A bird as big as this one means food for a few days, so my ancient provider's instinct is appeased. Now it's time to leave the rest alone to gobble and fight and breed and raise their broods undisturbed. I can tell you with equal certainty sometime late next February those charitable thoughts will fade, and I will dig out my turkey calls and start practicing again. Visions of parkerized 12-gauge magnum turkey guns will dance in my head, and I'll spend my idle hours plotting the demise of next year's tom. All of that lies several months in the future, however. Today I've got a lot of plucking to do.

Gobble, Gobble,
Philip

Chapter 7

MISSISSIPPI FLYWAY

Baton Rouge, LA

Dear Philip,

Yes we did. We got to participate in an American sporting legend, an Arkansas duck opening. Johnny Brenner's father, our senior host, didn't seem to think this year's opening was up to legend-making par, but I certainly made and missed enough shots to have got both excited and a sore shoulder. One of the shots I made, ordinary though it was, goes onto the Shots-I-Recall-With-Particular-Pleasure list.

It was actually the very first shot I took, down there in the timbered river bottom. John Senior and I were in the boat blind. You and Dave were across from us in one tree blind, Dave's father and Johnny in the tree blind to our left, and Uncle Fred was in his canoe, concealed and calling—it was his calling, everyone agreed, that made the day.

The first ducks had been dropped from those tree blinds and retrieved by Uncle Fred, when a single mallard drake came at me, straight overhead at medium range. It was a shot any capable gunner should make routinely, and what pleased me so was that I did just that: made it routinely, swinging up more or less without thought, hitting the bird with the center of my pattern so that it folded and dropped straight down, dead in the air. Didn't even flutter when it hit the water.

As you knew, I hadn't been duck hunting for several years, but I wouldn't have mentioned to you certain anxieties I had as to whether I belonged in that company of rice-farming, duck-powdering experts. To have a bird to myself, which made me an automatic center of attention for the moment, and to shoot it neatly and with ease, was pretty nice. And I was pleased that no one yelled "Good shot." In shooting, as in tennis, that's what gets said when the duffer hits a lucky one, unless it's genuinely brilliant, which mine so satisfactorily was not.

After that, I was able to settle down and enjoy the morning, and I did enjoy it a lot. Although, referring to the right shoulder, I think I've reached the age where a fellow hangs up his fancy 12-gauge and goes to, say, a Browning Light Twenty Automatic, with a 28-inch barrel and a 10-inch recoil pad.

A good part of the enjoyment, I would have to acknowledge, came from a certain kind of dumb pleasure fathers take in seeing their sons do almost anything well, and there were John Brenner, Steve Wilson, and I with smug grins on our faces as you and Dave and Johnny popped ducks. My use of the word *dumb*, above, has to do with many fathers' misconceptions that they have trained their boys right and got 'em out in the field. This is often nonsense, as illustrated by our particular case, since the son may well have taken the initiative, put the old gunner through a little subtle retraining, and kept the pressure on to get a hunt lined up. It was certainly the "C'mon, Dad" factor that put me in that boat blind at 5:45 in the morning. Hey, thanks.

Love,
Dad

. . .

Homestead, IA

Dear Dad,

There is, of course, no need to thank me, but I wish you'd given in to one more "C'mon, Dad" as in: "C'mon, Dad, you can cancel class and hunt with us this afternoon." Immediately after you left Arkansas, the flocks of mallards that had circled warily out of gun range all weekend while we shot teal and wigeons finally gave up and threw themselves onto the muzzles of blazing 16-gauge shotguns.

Before I go on to make you feel bad in some detail, let me be perfectly clear on one point: I missed the massacre, too, since I was eating lunch in the cab of John Brenner's pickup when the mallards committed mass, lemminglike suicide. What happened was, shortly after John drove you back to the cabin to pack for the trip home, Mr. Brenner, David and Steve Wilson and I gave up on the river bottom and drove twenty miles or so to a neighbor's place to hunt in his rice fields. It was a pretty big farm by Iowa standards—2,000 acres—but average, I guess, for the Grand Prairie of Arkansas. Two new brick houses, built as living quarters for the hired men and their families, stood side by side at the top of the lane, shaded by the only trees on the property. There was a big aluminum machine-shed next to the houses.

Somewhere along the way the lane turned into a levee, one of several that divided the property into ten floodable 160-acre fields, each one perfectly square and half a mile to a side. The fields are rotated between soybeans and rice, with one or two idled each year. The two idled fields had been flooded knee-deep for duck hunting, and there were one-man blinds built out in the middle. The field we began hunting in had five blinds: three in a row right in the middle and two more about 300 yards away. Both sets of blinds had huge, indifferently rigged spreads of mixed decoys— mallards, wood ducks, geese, whatever, all lumped together in big rafts. Numbers, apparently, are what you need here.

Dave and I volunteered to make the longer walk to the farthest two blinds. We still had a hundred yards to wade when Mr. Brenner and Steve Wilson reached the edge of their blocks, flushing a mallard drake who had been loafing unnoticed among the decoys. He dodged the hasty fusillade hurled in his direction and would have made good his escape had he not flown right to me, at eye level. He must have been looking back over his shoulder the whole time. That's how I shot my only mallard of the trip.

The blinds weren't much more than some kind of cane stuck in the mud, arranged in a ring just big enough to stand inside. Peeking through the stalks, you could see in all directions; there wasn't much chance of a duck's sneaking up on you out there if you stayed alert.

Anytime I looked straight up I would see, without fail, huge flocks of snow geese, way up high. I have no idea how many thousands of them there were, but one flock actually stretched unbroken from one horizon to the other. Slightly beneath the geese, large flocks of mallards flew purposefully toward distant rice fields. Smaller flocks would occasionally cup their wings and lose altitude gracefully, then look over our set, listen to Dave's inviting quacks, and say No, thank you.

The divers—redheads, bluebills, and ringnecks—kept us busy. They came in low over the water, bearing down on the decoys even after we leaned out of the blinds to shoot. Dave killed a limit of ducks in two seconds, doubling on redheads. I added a pair of bluebills and a ringneck to my mallard, and we were done for the day.

John arrived not long after, bringing with him several bags of cheeseburgers and french fries from a local diner. We left the blinds to eat lunch in the cab of the truck, which, like all farmers' pickups I've ever sat in, has a heater with two settings—"Off" and "91 degrees." The heat felt good, the food was pleasantly filling, and Dave told me a very long, involved, and quite interesting story about surf casting for stripers in New Jersey. A delightful stupor crept over me, so I leaned back in the seat and watched ducks and geese stream past out the window and felt about as content as a duck hunter can feel.

Meanwhile, Mr. Brenner was fretting. Time was running out and he meant to show at least one of his Yankee guests some real duck (read: mallard) hunting—I think he would as soon hunt field mice as diving ducks. He and Steve Wilson tried the other rice field, but the ducks wouldn't cooperate any better over there. In that situation you or I might re-arrange the decoys. Someone else might pick up all the shiny brass casings floating outside the blind and smear mud on his face to dull the shine. In Arkansas they find another caller. It happened that the two hired men were out doing something or other nearby. Mr. Brenner invited them into the blinds. Duck-hunting privileges being the major perk of their jobs, they had shotguns behind the seat of the pickup and duck calls in the glove compartment. They settled into the blinds, cranked out a few quacks, and that's all it took. Mallards poured in by the flock. All four of them shot limits; then they unloaded their guns and kept on calling in ducks just for fun until 3:00, when they had to quit so the Wilsons could drive to Memphis and catch a plane back to New York.

Said Steve Wilson, Wall Street attorney: "I always thought duck hunting was expensive, but here's this guy, he drives a combine for a living, has the best duck hunting I've ever seen in my life free, right behind his house, he's got the cost of one gun amortized over a lifetime, and he can kill three ducks with two shells."

For just a minute Steve looked like a man thinking about quitting the bar and learning a little bit about how to com-bine soybeans.

Mr. Brenner, who'd arranged for us to hunt with top callers all weekend only to see these two unknowns bring in the mallards for his guests at the last minute, was as flushed with excitement as if he'd come back from his first duck hunt.

"I guess they had the sound those ducks wanted to hear," was all he could say by way of explanation.

The sound, apparently, is "Quack," with a southern accent. I hope you get a chance to try it when those circling mallards reach Louisiana.

Love,
Philip

.　.　.

Baton Rouge, LA

Dear Philip,

When ducks are circling, I do not call, possibly because I have no Arkansas blood in my veins. I hold very still, look down at my feet, count to forty, and sneak a glance—here they come, or there they go. I'll have a chance, I think, to try this technique after Christmas, when my friend Cordell has invited me to go with him to his duck-lease in the western part of the state. Looking forward to it, I realize there has been a fundamental change in my hunting attitude.

By the time I stopped going out altogether, a few years back, I had rejected the sociability that goes along with hunting for most people—the guffaws and grits for breakfast, the yarn-spinning between shots, the critique and conventional funny excuses on the way home. (My favorite of the latter I first heard from an Iowa Conservation Commission guy named Bill, with whom I hunted pheasants once or twice, who used to say: "I couldn't hit my ass with either hand out there today.")

Instead of a sociable hunter, I had become, before quitting it, a determined loner, and the kind of experience I looked for in hunting happened very rarely.

Some of this may sound a little nutty. Probably it was, particularly the way it seems to have been influenced by particular dogs. I'd hunted some as a boy in Virginia with my brothers. We had .22s and we shot them at rabbits, squirrels, and groundhogs. But when I arrived in Iowa, the year you were born, I'd been living in dormitories, barracks, tents, or cities for twenty years, and didn't even own a gun. What I did own—I should say *we*—was Moon, the weimaraner, that beautiful, big, eerie-looking, green-eyed dog. Moon demanded a long daily run; there were shotguns available in the house we rented, there were pheasants, and sometimes quail, in the fields nearby, and ducks on the waters. And I had a couple of friends in Tom Williams and Dek Lardner who liked hunting more than casually. So everything came together there; even though we hadn't bought Moon for his hunting potential, I'd have to agree that his having it was catalytic. Maybe if we'd picked a greyhound, I'd have hung out at dog tracks.

It was probably the third year in Iowa, after Tom and Dek were gone, and when I was learning that I liked going out myself with Moon, that something occurred that seemed almost supernatural. I was in an abandoned, one-room wooden shack, with its door and windows long gone, at the edge of a remote pothole near the Iowa River. The dog and I had walked there in the dark on a stormy morning, lucky that we knew the way. I stood at the opening of what had been a big window, looking over the ten decoys I'd carried out in a gunnysack and then waded in and put in place. Light was coming gradually, without a sunrise. I heard a gun go off, far away.

Some ducks fluttered by quietly out of range, across the pothole from me. Because I was in a roofed building, not a blind, I couldn't see overhead or behind, but there were duck silhouettes moving across high, in front, and to the sides, and for several minutes I just enjoyed being where I was, protected from the weather, able to see without being seen, relaxing after what had been a long, cautious, burdensome walk in hip boots to get there.

And a duck materialized. Damn it, he did. In the empty

space in front of me there had been nothing, nor to the right, nor to the left. Now there was a duck, flying without forward motion, and a gun raising itself to my shoulder as the duck increased gradually in size until there was no way the gun could miss it, no way it could fail to drop, no way Moon could avoid gliding by me out the window and into the water to retrieve. I'm almost ready to claim he didn't make a splash, but then I'd have to claim that he was perfectly dry when he brought the duck in through the open door space, and you might not believe my magic moment ever was.

I think it was starting then that duck hunting became a passion rather than a pastime for me. A magic moment might come only once or twice a season. It might not come at all. But to have any chance for one, I had to be out alone with Moon. Solitude, stillness, strange weather, difficulty, and the kind of empty-minded relaxation that is really the highest form of concentration were part of the spell that could make this thing happen, and there were, I think, certain incantatory patterns, if not actual charm-words, that must not be interrupted. In what now seems to me an absurd way, I was something like a spiritual man waiting for his next mystical experience, and what a burden that was to place on a rather crude, atavistic, outdoor activity.

I was in Iowa twenty-two years. Every season, as those years went on, there were fewer ducks and more hunters. A place both likely and isolated was hard to find, and Moon died, to be replaced by Bix, the springer. Bix hadn't a jot of the spooky intensity that made Moon so fit a partner for enchantment. I don't think you ever hunted with Bix. You probably remember him as a dumb, affectionate clown of a dog, and so he was. But in the field he had another quality, which was hardheaded stubbornness. He never gave up once he was quartering or trailing a dead or wounded bird. You just couldn't call him off, working at that gait we called lolloping, with a grin on his face and his tail wagging as if it were motorized.

Hunting with Bix, you had to laugh at him, and it was hard to take yourself quite seriously, either.

In Bixie's second season I stayed home Opening Day for the first time in something like fifteen years. The duck population was really down, according to the papers, and the Coralville Reservoir Refuge was attracting whatever local and migrant birds there were. That meant hunters would be shoulder to shoulder along the refuge boundary, taking pass shots at high ducks with very little chance of retrieving those they hit. I didn't want to see those hunters or hear them. The Opening was, as usual, on a Saturday morning. I didn't go to the reservoir until late Sunday afternoon. I took Bix and no gun. We started off along some car tracks, through corn stubble that led to flooded timber, and hadn't gone more than a hundred yards from the car before I heard an indignant quack, and saw Bix dragging a wing-and-neck-shot pintail hen out of a brush pile. He brought her over, and I dispatched her. She was not a bird that would have healed. Fox food.

It took Bix about forty-five minutes to collect a limit of crippled ducks for me. I was proud of the dog, ashamed of the hunters; so I quit waterfowling for a while, but I missed it. And now I'm going back out when the company is going to be congenial, liking the sociability that I avoided in the days of the dog named Moon. Let's hope to be back with our friends in Arkansas next year.

Love,
Dad

. . .

Homestead, IA

Dear Dad:

If dogs tell the whole story of what and how we hunt, then certainly Sam has more than a little to do with why I don't hunt ducks. With his short coat he can't sit still in the cold, and since he refuses to swim anyway, there's really no reason to take him duck hunting at all. Instead of spooky intensity or affectionate clownishness, Sam has only a certain high-strung excitability that endears him to no one but me. Most of his life is spent waiting to go hunting, so I feel guilty chasing ducks or deer or whatever if bird season is open. Perhaps, as you pointed out in the case of Moon and your own hunting, if someone had given me a Lab instead of a German shorthair, I'd hunt ducks instead of birds.

Sam is not the whole story. There are less and less ducks in these days of drought and high-yield farming. Unless the setting is perfect, as it was in Arkansas, I don't feel good about killing even just a few of them. On my last Opening Day at the reservoir two or three years ago, I did, however, see what passes for a great moment in modern waterfowling. Six or seven guys, good, patient hunters and excellent callers, had staked out a small pond on the mud flats near a slough lined with Opening Day skybusters. The hunters around the pond were able to convince about one duck in every three that their little willow-lined pothole was situated precisely in the calm eye of the lead storm raging over the marsh.

What made it impressive, though, was how the pond guys managed to bully the slough guys into letting the ducks come all the way in. There'd be a lot of blasting, then a duck would show a little interest in the pond. He'd set his wings and curve out over the slough. Dire and sincere stage-whispered threats followed, and, more often than not, an uneasy cease-fire descended over the marsh. All eyes would turn to the duck, circling lower and lower, unaware of the fistfights he was nearly provoking on the ground, until, BANG—down he went, cleanly killed and floating on the surface of the pond. Then the pass shooters would open up again. I was impressed, but I haven't been back for a duck opening since.

It's still possible, I think, to go on the kind of hunt I like around here. The way it's done—and this is a kind of duck hunting you never seemed to care for—is to buy a big boat blind, the kind often equipped with bunk beds, stoves, and sometimes even televisions for football Saturdays. As I understand it, you go out at midnight on big water somewhere and find a good spot, sleep until a couple of hours before shooting light. Then you cook breakfast and rig one of those huge rafts of decoys that make waterfowling into a project about what I imagine commercial fishing to be like.

There are a lot of boat blinds for sale in these days of thirty-day seasons and three-bird limits. Sometimes I think I'd like to buy one if I could afford it and learn to handle the big boat in the dark, spend time repainting and maintaining all those decoys in the off-season, even get good at backing up boat trailers. And it would be worth doing, too, just for the chance to get out among the ducks by yourself.

So long as I keep trying to write for a living, I won't be flush enough to buy a duck boat anytime soon. Meanwhile there's Sam, who, as I've said, lives to hunt, and duck season coincides with the woodcock flights and the best part of pheasant season. Compared to the cost of duck hunting gear (or the cost of anything these days), bird hunting is dirt cheap: I need only a whistle, boots, a gun, half a dozen shells, and enough gas to drive—at most—ten miles down the road to find a place to hunt. At those prices, Sam and I will stick with birds, thanks, until it's time to go to Arkansas again.

Love,
Philip

• • •

Baton Rouge, LA

Dear Philip,

We do seem to be circling like mallards around saying some sort of farewell to duck hunting, and, like mallards, could both probably be decoyed and called back to the blinds as I was the other day by my friend Cordell. Southwest Louisiana is where he called from, bidding me to his duck-lease over a big saltwater marsh on the Gulf coast. So, I realize, I completed (slowly, over half a lifetime), the cycle of Mississippi Flyway hunting. I've been from the nesting grounds in Canada through some of the celebrated hotspots—the Saskatchewan wheat fields; the Illinois River bottoms once with Dek; Cairo, Illinois; Swan Lake, Missouri; our Arkansas duck opening—and now the wintering grounds.

This last was a pleasant hunt, rather than a great one, but more than that, one hell of a bird show, featuring unbelievable numbers of large white and off-white birds, with black decorations on most of them. Accompanying me and Cordell, who is a lawyer, were Bill, one of his former law-school teachers, and, not unreasonably, their two sons, boys a good deal younger than the sons of the three old guys who appeared in my earlier letter.

Finding and engaging the right duck-lease is a serious matter in Louisiana, a sportsman's paradise generally reserved for the affluent or people who do business with the oil companies, and, at the rural end of the stick, for Cajuns (of whom it is said we could have easily won the war in Vietnam if we'd sworn in a squad of them and told them that the Viet Cong were good to eat, but that they were out of season and there was a limit of two on them). In Cordell's marsh we heard guns go off a few times in the distance but saw no one else all day long.

Do you recall a discussion we once had concerning Tennessee Mick Angel's calling a splitting maul a *go-devil?* Once, during one of those idle moments with a dictionary, I found six other uses for the term: an alligator, a handcar, a hay sweep, a pipeline-cleaning device, an iron dart dipped into an oil well to explode dynamite, and a certain kind of cultivator. Now I've got an eighth. It's an outboard motor with a very long, outward-tilting shaft to propel a small boat through shallow water, and used, on the first morning of our hunt, to propel Bill and the two boys to the first of the two blinds we used, and then Cordell and me to the other.

This kind of go-devil is also excellent for flushing aforementioned large birds off the water, of which we saw, wheeling and turning pink in the sunrise, white pelicans, great egrets, snowy egrets, white ibis, a wood stork (I was amazed; I think she got up off a nest rather than the water); and then, truly astonishing and in no need of a sunrise to pink them, roseate spoonbills. It was absolutely beautiful, and, except for the stork, these birds were in crowds, filling the air, climbing and turning.

There was one final white bird that didn't have the sense to flee the go-devil at all. He was roosted out in front of the prefab plastic blind Cordell and I got into, a blind sitting on mud in shallow water, and we were all set and loaded, looking for ducks, when this last white bird decided it was flying time. It rose fifty yards out and flew directly at us, and I watched, trying to decide which of the various kinds it might be. Head on, it was all wings and body, with no discernible shape.

Then it made a turn to cross in front of us, left to right, and I said, "Cordell, that can't be a snow goose, can it?"

"It sure can," he said. "Shoot it."

By now the bird was in profile, and very clearly a goose. It was also in front of Cordell, on the right and going away from me. I didn't want to fire across my host's chin, though, for one thing, and for another, I had sixes in my little 12-gauge while Cordell had 3-inch magnums.

"You take him," I said, and Cordell dropped the bird with one, clean shot, waded out, and brought in the goose. That was our retrieving style: waders, and a gun carried out in one hand in case a bird was crippled, which was not the condition of that snow goose.

After that we heard the boys and Bill shooting a lot and had a few wild chances to ourselves, but I don't think I hit my first duck until an hour or so later, when we switched blinds. I don't have any idea why almost all of the action was at the first one, but when I joined Bill (and Cordell took the boys off, where they got into snipe) the ducks did start swinging in over the decoys at nice ten- and fifteen-minute intervals.

They were mostly green-winged teal, which came bursting into range but never slowed down, and gadwalls, which did tend to drop in. There wasn't a mallard to be seen, and the only other species in the bag when we went in around eleven was a couple of widgeons, and, I'm sorry to say, a canvasback.

The lawyers conferred and pointed out that, since leaving him behind wouldn't revive him, we might as well have him dressed out with the rest.

In the afternoon, we took a drive through a nearby refuge, and the show there was put on by fine collections of shore-birds, gulls and terns, plenty more pelicans, and remarkable numbers of kingfishers watching from the wires.

I brooded a little about the canvasback driving home. Obviously, no one meant to shoot it, and I'm not sure which of us did. But there'll come a time, unless some really massive effort goes into habitat restoration, when the illegal species will be several. Hen mallards, redheads, woodies—all the hundred-point ducks—and I expect pintails and black ducks, too. And I'm going to have to say that I'm just not certain enough at in-flight identification to be comfortable in a duck blind if there are six or seven species out there in such short supply as to be illegal.

I think when the fathers of the next generation start their sons off, it better be with binoculars before they move on to shotguns, unless evolution provides them with telephoto eyes.

I wouldn't have missed my shooting years up and down the flyway. They've meant a lot to me, but I can't tell myself that the stamps I bought and the money I once raised for Ducks Unlimited offset my lifetime bag, although it was hardly one of the great ones. And I do love to eat those birds, perhaps the best of any meat there is. But I think waiting and watching is the next attitude for me; maybe with some wet years, strict limits, strong enforcement, and a big push for habitat, the ducks will come back. And if they do, maybe I will, too.

Love,
Dad

Chapter 8

VENISON

Note enclosed in UPS second-day-air box: Dear Dad: Here's some venison salami from the Kalona Locker; hope it arrives okay. Also note photo of me, bow, and defunct deer.

Enjoy,
Philip

. . .

Baton Rouge, LA

Dear Philip,

Thanks for the salami and the photo of the handsome, horned creature. When it comes to red meat, there is nothing even close to venison in my salivating opinion, the marinated haunch well roasted (do not omit juniper berries from the marinade); the chops, the steaks, and wonderful livers. Have you any left in the freezer? I ask because here among the Cajuns there is a preparation called *Venison Grillades* that is stupendously good, and for which I will search out a recipe if you still have meat to cook it with.

Love,
Dad

. . .

Homestead, IA

Dear Dad,

Glad you liked the salami and photo, although you should know that deer are antlered (which I realize does not alliterate nicely with "handsome" but is biologically correct), not horned. The details of my hunt, which I neglected to include, are remarkably few—my archery season lasted only two days this year. I didn't hunt at all until three weeks after the season opened October 1, although I'd spent some time finding a good place to put my stand. The first afternoon I hunted, I saw nine deer in range, although none were bucks. Since it was only my first day out, and all of the does had fawns with them, I didn't draw the bow.

Two days later I climbed back into the stand at 5:00 P.M., and it wasn't twenty minutes later that a buck, identifiable as such by a modest eight-point rack, materialized twenty-five yards to my right, chewing on some long grass. He walked in a leisurely circle three-quarters of the way around the stand, unaware of my presence ten feet off the ground. I'd put the stand at the bottom of a hill, knowing that the cooling afternoon air would make my scent sink, not rise, so deer descending the hillside wouldn't smell me until they passed the stand.

The buck was headed eventually for the cornfield across the creek, but he was taking his time, nibbling leaves, pausing here and there to whack a sapling with his antlers, so as not to arrive in the open too long before dark. I tried to calm myself with the thought that he wouldn't ever really come into range; like a lot of hunters I'm afflicted with near-disabling surges of buck fever when a deer I plan to convert into chops walks to within shooting distance.

The buck finally did step too close for me to pretend I wasn't going to shoot anymore, and by now he was walking quickly, so I didn't have time to get nervous. I drew the bow and shot him through the ribs at fifteen yards as if I shot deer every day. Never mind that it had been three whole seasons of getting up early, waiting long hours, freezing in a tree, and missing and spooking deer since the last time I killed a buck with my bow.

Like most corn-eating northern bucks, this was a big one—I got nearly 100 pounds of chops, steaks, kabobs back from the locker, plus the salami. The venison should last until May or so, when the pheasants, woodcock, miscellaneous birds, and rabbits all run out at once, just about the same time teaching assistants stop getting paid for the summer. We'll then live in a state of economically enforced semi-vegetarianism until fall. My ability with bow and shotgun has never stood between my family and starvation, and I hope it never has to, but venison has saved us from a whole lot of macaroni and cheese over the years. Glad I could send some meat your way. I'll save some of mine for *grillades*.

Love,
Philip

. . .

Baton Rouge, LA

Dear Philip:

If you have to live a semi-vegetarian life part of the time, summer is the part to do it. Garden time in Iowa. Vine-ripened tomatoes, fresh snow peas, tiny, tender-skinned new potatoes. Add that amazing fresh-picked Iowa sweet corn. I suppose I was better at providing those red, white, green, and yellow alternatives to macaroni when I lived on the farm than at delivering venison, but if I'd known about *grillades*, I might have tried harder.

I am caught, on my way to the kitchen with you, by the thought that my deer hunting may have lacked intensity for a reason quite different from the one I used to give myself, which was that I simply preferred to spend my field time hunting birds. There was, I think, along with that, some kind of disbelief that I'd ever get a deer, something like the feeling I've had looking at a big, unfamiliar lake: that I'd never be able to catch a fish out of a place like that. I'm inclined to credit you with changing my mind.

A little later in this correspondence, when I've had a chance to sort through thoughts and recollections of deer hunting prior to the one deer I got (since when I've not hunted deer), I'll circle back to this, but now let's cook.

The *grillades* recipe here is the one Ava Haymon served when I came in, very hungry, from that duck hunt with Cordell. I couldn't believe anything could be that good. I've cooked it two or three times since, pretty much like this:

2 pounds venison, cut in 1- and 2-inch chunks
Butter, bacon fat, or vegetable oil
¼ cup flour
1 cup chopped onions (use part shallots if you have them)
½ cup chopped celery
1 cup chopped bell pepper
1 clove garlic, chopped fine
Medium tomato, chopped
Pinch of tarragon
½ tsp. thyme
½ cup brown stock or beef broth
½ cup red wine
1 bay leaf
Salt, pepper, Tabasco, and Worcestershire sauce to taste
Chopped parsley

Brown the meat in whichever of the fats your doctor lets you use, in an iron casserole or deep skillet for which you have a tight lid. (It can be transferred to a crockpot once all the ingredients are combined.) Remove meat and set aside. Add flour and more fat to the pan, enough to make a brown roux. When roux is ready, add onions, celery, peppers, and garlic, and cook until the onions are soft and transparent. Add tomato, tarragon, and thyme, and cook a bit more. Add stock and wine. Add meat, salt, pepper, bay leaf (removed later), Tabasco, Worcestershire. Learn how to spell Worcestershire *by copying from bottle. Cover and simmer until meat is fork tender, which will take a couple of hours (or more). Let stand a while before serving. (The* Plantation Cookbook *says "several hours or overnight in the refrigerator.") Take out the bay leaf and put in the parsley before reheating.*

I recommend making a much larger amount than specified above, so as to be able to divide into packages and freeze. I don't know why it should be so, but venison and venison dishes always seem to me to be improved by freezing, so long, that is, as one does not forget to thaw.

Grillades are served over grits down here, and I don't believe there's anything in the Articles of Surrender signed by Robert E. Lee that says you can't serve them over grits up there.

Love,
Dad

. . .

Homestead, IA

Dear Dad:

Thanks for the recipe. I've always eaten grits with butter and maple syrup—a sure hanging offense, I've been told by indignant Southerners, had Grant surrendered to Lee—but I promise to whip up some *grillades* instead, next time I feel like eating Southern.

Venison aside, I didn't use to care all that much for deer season myself, but for different reasons than your own. By the time I started deer hunting there were enough deer, and our neighborhood hunt was well enough organized, that our Opening Day drive always produced meat for everyone. The way we hunted never appealed to me, and I didn't really understand what all the fuss over deer hunting was about. Our farmer-neighbors chased deer through the woods like lost livestock. When the does and small bucks gullible enough to run past our tree stands appeared, I shot them without compunction or excitement. It seemed too easy to count as real hunting, but the meat was good, so I pulled the trigger when the time came.

It wasn't until I bought a bow and started hunting by myself that I really started to enjoy deer hunting. During my first archery season I saw very few deer, and those I did see either saw, heard, or smelled me first, and I finally began to realize just how tightly wound and wary whitetails are. That year I learned to enjoy being invisible to the other residents of the woodlots I hunted, and I always looked forward to watching the nightshift of coons, owls, and possums go to bed while the hawks, songbirds, and squirrels went to work in the morning. Climbing into my tree stand in the mornings, I felt like another member of the dayshift, accepted by the others as a clumsy arboreal predator too big to eat and not particularly dangerous, although the occasional squirrel would take me to task just for being there.

During the gun season that year I hunted by myself whenever I could sneak away from the organized drives. Late one afternoon, stalking quietly over fresh snow with the wind in my face, I was able to tiptoe to within fifteen feet of an unsuspecting buck and shoot him. Deer hunting took on a whole new meaning for me then, as an exercise in skill, patience, and stealth, not just driving and shooting and looking for lost drivers and pulling pickups out of the mud.

I've heard that venison from unalarmed deer is supposed to taste better than meat from deer who've been spooked and are running, because the former deer are not pumped full of adrenaline. I don't know if that's the reason, but the meat does taste better to me when I know I've brought it home all by myself.

Love,
Philip

. . .

Baton Rouge, LA

Dear Philip,

Yes, I agree about our Opening Day deer drives, in which I used to take part before I left the farm. It was more like harvesting than hunting, or a team sport with too many captains. Generally, my position was driver—I'd get cold and bored sitting in a stand, and though I remember taking a wild shot or two, it was usually at a deer I jumped, moving at take-off speed. I was never the guy who knocked down one of the ones we shared, until my last deer hunt. Last, it's likely, in both senses.

Indulge me in one more paragraph of venison thoughts, and I will lay down knife and fork and pick up gun.

First, I always used to amaze our farmer cohorts by the intensity with which I searched out the kidneys when we field-dressed (they knew all about the heart and liver); of all the kidneys I have eaten, deer have the finest. I also amazed them by asking that one haunch be kept whole for me instead of getting sliced into small steaks and roasts; expanding on my first letter, my notion of the supreme festive offering for fifteen to twenty dinner guests is a haunch of venison, soaked for twenty-four hours in a cooked marinade of red wine, onions, garlic, leeks, juniper berries, celery, salt, pepper, and parsley, roasted medium rare and sliced quite thin.

What perplexed them most was my having a cup and plastic container along one day at field-dressing time, with which to catch and carry off a pint of blood; the week before I'd read that Paul Bocuse, the great chef, who'd arrived in New York to cook an important dinner, intended to thicken his sauce with blood instead of flour or cornstarch. Tried it that evening on a sauce *poivrade*. Worked delicious. (As you probably know, you must keep the temperature of the sauce being thickened under the boiling point, or everything curdles.)

You may (but there's no reason that you should) remember

that I'd left the farm by the time I killed my only deer. I was there briefly for a visit. We had the usual farmer friends, but I knew straight off it was going to be different because you provided me with a gun with sights. I was never a natural shotgun shot, but could (and, I expect, from infantry training, still can) handle a rifle well enough, so your putting that nifty little sighted shotgun in my hands was one of the supreme moments of "C'mon, Dad."

On the morning of the second day that year I drove. I didn't get a shot, but in the middle of the afternoon we various captains decided to cross the Rohret Road and hunt Ronnie Loan's cornfields. I was the first to be let out of the pickup and had totally vague directions as to where to go. I walked up a hedgerow, and saw enough tracks and fresh droppings at a particular point to persuade me that deer were using it as the way through the hedgerow. I backed up, decided where to hide myself, and cleared fields of fire in both directions. I didn't know where anyone else might be, who was driving, who was on stands. It didn't matter. I liked the solitude.

It was misty, a somber afternoon, and very, very quiet. I waited twenty minutes, wondering where the rest of you had gone. I think it was because I had confidence in the gun that I kept alert, there in the gray silence. And along came the deer, appearing blurred and soundlessly at first, the ground was so damp.

First came three does, running in nice, controlled leaps, no panic. Then a young spike buck, fourth in line, bounding the same way. They were very graceful, moving that way; they became clear, and there was no question in my mind of missing a shot as I raised the gun, sighted behind the buck's near shoulder, and took him in midair. All four feet were off the ground, and since he fell on his side, I'm not sure any foot ever touched again.

I knew for the first and only time what it is that makes deer hunters love their sport. I'd put it together myself, for the first time. Figured out where to be, set myself up properly, waited for the right moment and shot well.

That was my half-minute of being a deer hunter, because next I did something that showed profound and dopey inexperience. Remembering tales of deer knocked down, getting up, and running off, I walked halfway to my buck and shot it in the head unnecessarily. He was well killed by the first shot, and I remember your saying as you arrived—for those deer had heard truck doors closing or something and trotted off before you started your drive—"I heard the first shot and told the guys, 'Dad got one.' When I heard the second shot, I said, 'Well, maybe he didn't.'"

That exhausts my sparse store of deer-hunting stories, but there's one of yours I'd like to know about. You were uncommunicative about it at the time. It began the same day my deer-hunting life began and probably ended, and it convinced me that yours would be illustrious. Walking home we jumped a big wounded buck out of some giant horseweeds on the Eckerman place, took shots ourselves, and hit him. But he was moving fast and went quickly out of sight at a high-speed limp.

We trailed him—or you did, and I walked along—over the steep ridge by the schoolhouse, down the other side, across the Black Diamond Road, across our soybean field, to Old Man's Creek, where it looked as if he'd slid down the bank and swum across. But when we got to the other side, the sign was much less clear. We had taken a dog, I think, though I don't recall which one, hoping for help in picking up a trail. We didn't get much. Darkness came, and we went in.

But the next morning you got up and went out by yourself, not saying much about it, and were back by noon, saying that you'd found the buck, would I give you a hand dragging him home. How on earth did you do it?

Love,
Dad

• • •

Homestead, IA

Dear Dad,

I'm glad you had one chance to find out that there is a good deal to like about deer hunting once you get off by yourself. There is much to be done right, from picking a stand to shooting to dressing to, as we have discussed at some length, cooking. Demonstrating competence in a major food-gathering endeavor, I think, lies at the heart of deer hunting's appeal for many people—it's the same impulse that leads some to hard-core gardening and others to serious berry picking.

Shooting well at the right time is one of the most important skills in deer hunting, although the better you've done everything else, the easier the shooting should be. You shot well when you killed your deer, and you shouldn't kick yourself for shooting him again; it's better to kill them too dead than not dead enough, which was the problem with that buck on the creek bottom you asked me about.

I was uncommunicative on the day you remember because looking for wounded deer always puts me in a bad mood, pestered by the knowledge that if someone (in this case me) hadn't messed up, I wouldn't have to be tracking the deer at all. Also, as you may have forgotten, the season had actually ended at sunset the previous day, so what I did that morning was not entirely legal, but I felt guilty and responsible enough for the pain I'd caused to take the small risk that I'd be caught by the game warden. I took my gun, a knife, some slugs, and half a dozen high-brass #5s—I think I had some lame idea I would toss the slugs and tell anyone who asked that I was pheasant hunting if I had to—and left the house early.

Going to the spot where I thought the buck had crossed the creek, I crawled on my hands and knees in ever-widening circles until I found a drop of blood. I marked it with my orange hat, and made circles around that until I found another drop. Then I found one more, far from the others, but in a straight enough line to let me know which way the deer was traveling. I followed the easiest path, as a wounded deer often will, to a hiding place—a stand of thick willows. Although I knew he was probably in there, I might not have seen him before he saw me if his antlers hadn't been so big, and glinting in the sunlight. I kneeled and took the only shot the bedded buck offered: through the neck at about eighty yards.

The nine-point rack, which I had mounted, dwarfs all the others lying around the house. My first slug had hit him under the eye, the result of an ill-chosen head shot I tried when we first jumped him. I think he might have survived that, but his smashed shoulder, the injury we'd first noticed, would have become infected and killed him eventually. It wasn't a bullet wound, by the way. He must have been hit by a car or caught his leg in a fence earlier in the week.

The other night, speaking of deer hit by cars, I told the sheriff's deputy I didn't want the doe someone hit on the road in front of my house. He took it away to be dressed and fed to the inmates at the county jail. Some people, he told me, buy police scanners just to listen for reported roadkills, and pick up four or five deer a year that way. I said I'd rather shoot my own, thanks. Deer hunting means more to me than just venison—although without venison it would mean nothing at all—even if you and I can't ever seem to talk for very long without bringing that part up.

Love,
Philip

Chapter 9

─────

MISCELLANEOUS BIRDS

Homestead, IA

Dear Dad,

I was out in Nebraska last week, looking over the new Cabela's store for *Sports Afield*, and on my second and last afternoon there the nice PR folks took me dove hunting. I really enjoyed the solitude of the Nebraska plains and the mild, dry weather that made an overturned bucket underneath a windmill seem like exactly the right place to be sitting. Unfortunately the flight, such as it was, lasted from about 4:00 to 4:30, during which time a total of four doves flew by. My host shot one; I missed the first bird that came barreling past with the wind under his tail while I fumbled with the right-handed safety on my borrowed autoloader, then killed the second, which was perhaps the single dimmest dove in western Nebraska. That second bird came into the windmill while we were taking a root beer break. He flared when he saw us, but then circled in a holding pattern long enough for me to set my pop down without spilling a drop, run around to the far side of the windmill, pick up the gun, figure out the safety, and shoot him after he obligingly turned around to beat back upwind, making himself into a more or less stationary target.

What with this windmill representing the only water for miles around, I'd have thought we'd see more than four doves. The rest must already be on their way to Louisiana. Get ready. Meanwhile, now that I'm back home, where doves are protected and pheasants not due to open for another month, I'm thinking it might be nice to get out again. My early season bird-hunting choices are confined to early, resident woodcock, early snipe or rails, all migratory birds without webbed feet—a category that would include doves, too, I suppose.

Sometimes I do wish we had a dove season here, since there is the occasional balmy September afternoon that would be just right for sitting near a pond, pulling on a Mountain Dew, and waiting for the evening flight.

> Love,
> Philip

.   .   .

Baton Rouge, LA

Dear Philip,

Your soft-spoken wish for an Iowa dove season is one about which I spoke loudly and firmly some years back, thus almost becoming the father of legal Iowa dove-hunting. I was, I think, one issue of the *Des Moines Register* away from getting it done.

I'd been over to Illinois a number of times, not just for the opening days but for follow-up days, and I just loved being able to do all that shooting. From which you may conclude the flights were larger and longer than the four birds that the nice Cabela's people may have imported and released for you. Do you suppose the one that hovered so obligingly was trained?

A likelier probability is that the clean farming over there has wiped out that great favorite among dove foods, the hemp plant, grown during World War II in the midwest for rope and since gone wild and widespread. It looks, tastes, and smells just like its first cousin, the marijuana plant. (My old, lamented friend John Pearson couldn't believe it wasn't; he dried some, rolled it and smoked it, and said, sadly, "In Iowa they've got 3.2 pot.")

The doves are crazy about the seeds, though whether that has anything more than food value for them, I dunno. If so, it may explain a remark you made when I first took you and your gun across the river.

"I don't see why people think doves are meek and mild," you said. "They seem quite dashing to me, like those French World War I aviators who went tearing through the sky in soft leather helmets with silk scarves around their necks."

But I didn't quote you—nor J. Pearson either—when I went off to the state capitol. A lobbyist for the Izaak Walton League (was it Pete Russell?) went with me, but thought he'd better stay low on this one since he had a number of other bills to work on that spring. But he did provide me with some information, and with introductions to some professionals on the Conservation Commission, who told me they were all for a dove season, had sponsored an enabling bill themselves a couple of seasons back, and had seen it shattered like a clay pigeon. They weren't going to sponsor again, but they put me in touch with some sympathetic legislators on (if I have the title right) the House Fish and Game Committee.

Perhaps the most unexpected—certainly most per-suasive—argument I found was that the Audubon Society didn't oppose dove hunting. The reason was that the big concentration of birds in the most populous roosts could lead to epidemics of a certain fatal dove disease, transmitted from the parents to the young while feeding by inserting adult beaks into juvenile throats. The food, which as I recall is called dove's milk, is in liquid form, the liquid being created by the parent in, I guess, the craw. In dove-hunting states, starting with the first shots on Opening Day, the big flocks begin to scatter out, forming smaller flocks and using a much wider assortment of roosts. Made for healthy birds.

The Committee guys loved that one.

Late in the afternoon, feeling off to a good start, I went to see the managing editor of the *Register*, then even more than now the state newspaper. He was cordial, knew who I was, was glad to meet me, and said as follows: that the *Register* wouldn't support a dove bill; the reason we didn't have a season was because a good many of the Iowa religious fundamentalists considered the dove an important Christian symbol. On the other hand, he assured me, the *Register* didn't think the matter a particularly important one and would pay it very little attention.

Okay. A few days later, I got a call from one of my Conservation Commission friends. He told me the gents on our legislative committee had a bill ready, and would, that day, report it out as a Committee bill, which meant that they were unanimous and enthusiastic. We should have a pretty good chance with the full House and Senate, and the governor—it was Harold Hughes in his second term—was a hunter himself.

Went to bed feeling good about it. Could hardly wait for the mail the next day; it would have the newspaper in it, in which I expected to find some nice, obscure, undamaging coverage. I can't quote the headline, but it was an actual banner across the top of Page One, seven columns of bold type, like they would have used if we'd declared war on China. This will be fairly close to the wording:

HOUSE COMMITTEE SPONSORS IOWA DOVE-HUNTING SEASON

It was illustrated with a large photograph of the last passenger pigeon.

Did I say something about shattered birds?

After that, each year—and I rely on the statute of limitations and the lack of an extradition treaty between Iowa and Louisiana covering the crime—I annually declared for myself a Secret, Illegal, One-Day Iowa Dove Season, arbitrarily holding it on whatever fine day I liked, and had some nice shoots on various secluded places around the farm.

I remember one in particular, a mild Christmas morning after present-opening and breakfast, when I sat in a sunny hollow out of the wind, doves moving above me across an open space between a row of old pear trees and some big pines they liked to sit in. I was shooting well—we had doves for Christmas lunch—and I don't even feel guilty about it now, although perhaps I should.

I think it was in the lobbying year that I discovered snipe were legal, and that no one but me seemed to want to hunt them, which is probably what kept my personal dove season down to a single day.

Love,
Dad

. . .

Homestead, IA

Dear Dad,

Your illegal dove-season secret is safe with me, and I suppose you, as the almost-father of Iowa dove hunting, deserved to celebrate a one-day season if anyone did. I'm sure, by the way, that I never said that about the doves with scarves, although I wouldn't be surprised if the bird I shot in Nebraska was feeling no pain as he circled the windmill.

My Illinois dove hunting didn't last more than two outings. I accompanied the Lardners to public-area dove openings near Keithsburg twice—the first I rather enjoyed, although I suspect a significant part of the damage my right ear has suffered thanks to gunfire occurred in that one day. I shot all four boxes of shells I brought plus some goose loads I found deep in the pockets of your old duck-hunting coat. Once I'd run out of 12-gauge loads, the Lardners gave me a 20- and some more shells so I could keep going. I must have shot, oh, 125 to 150 rounds without earplugs, nearly winding up with a 12-bird limit and almost certainly winding up with some permanent hearing loss.

What made that first hunt fun was that we had a good spot more or less to ourselves, and although there were many, many people hunting doves on the state-owned land, none were really in sight of us, since the area was made up of several small fields with trees surrounding each one. The next year, however, there were even more people, quite a few of whom decided it would be all right with us if they shared the sunflower field we'd surrounded. I wore earplugs this time and my shooting was better, but I was put off by the mob of shooters. If I ever really made this alleged French aviator/dove remark, it must have been prompted by the aerobatics I saw the doves performing that day once the guns began to go off. If they were French aviators, we on the ground represented more anti-aircraft fire than the Germans mustered in both wars put together. Hunting, I decided early in the shoot, makes very little sense when you have to root for a bird to get past everyone else so you can kill it.

That was my last Opening Day, and the problem with dove hunting in Illinois (theoretically), Iowa, and, it would seem, western Nebraska, is that the big flocks of doves don't stick around much past the opening, opting for warmer climes as soon as the first good cold snap arrives in September. So I haven't been out since those opening days in Keithsburg, until just the other week, near Sidney, NE.

For several years I replaced the Illinois dove opening with the Iowa snipe opening on my hunting calendar. Finally I decided that marching around river-bottom muck in 90-degree heat was really no more my idea of good fun than was standing shoulder to shoulder with people I didn't know and shooting at doves.

By mid- to late October, however, as the weather cools and the flight birds arrive, along with various other interesting-to-watch migratory birds, snipe hunting approaches the idyllic. No one chases them across the Road O'

Mud Flats but me, and I can bang away to my heart's content at flight birds. One absolutely perfect fall day I actually shot an eight-bird limit with much less than a box of shells, including a double on birds seven and eight. It was a performance with a shotgun that would have qualified me for living legend status had there been witnesses, and had I the good sense to quit wing-shooting forever right then and there.

Love,
Philip

. . .

Baton Rouge, LA

Dear Philip,

I don't quite know why snipe, rather than woodcock, which are more comical to look at, should be the supposed target in a classical American prank. I do know that when I asked a friend or two my age whether he'd like to go snipe hunting, the answer was, "Oh, sure. You bet. I'll bring my left-handed monkey wrench."

As I recall it from reading *The Adventures of Pinky Pinkerton*, as serialized in *St. Nicholas* back issues (it was a nineteenth-century kids' magazine, of which my mother was fond, which is why we had bound back issues), snipe hunting was inflicted on the gullible as follows: You equipped your victims with a sack and two rocks. The rock man was supposed to beat his weapons together, thus attracting snipe into the sack held open by the other guy. This went on at night, the time, as everybody knows, when snipe are unable to resist the attraction of rocks beaten together.

It's hard to believe that kids went for this, but then I trust you will find it equally hard to believe what happened to me the last time I went snipe hunting down here. I had just bought this new, geriatric 20-gauge, see, and I wanted to pattern it. Saw a pile of junk in one corner of the field, with a fair-sized piece of cardboard in it, which was just the thing to fire at. I then strolled over, gun in hand, to retrieve and inspect the cardboard without really looking very closely. If I had, I'd have realized that the junk was there in order to start filling a hole, and that hole was full of water. Went in up to my waist. Wet shells, mud in muzzle. Things like that just don't happen when you hunt woodcock.

Love,
Dad

. . .

Homestead, IA

Dear Dad,

I'm afraid I find it entirely plausible, even in character, for you to have plunged into some kind of sinkhole while snipe hunting. Heck, I've seen you do it.

As a child, I probably never would have fallen for the snipe-hunting trick, since I knew you snipe-hunted and had seen you come back covered in mud with funny-looking birds in hand. On the other hand, I might have said: "You're kidding—there's a way to hunt snipe without falling into the mud? I'll have to tell my dad."

Most of my snipe hunts were pretty wet and muddy, too.

I might add here that the classic snipe-hunt format, as you described it, can be raised to heights of elegant complexity when staged by practical jokers of the right sort. Dek Lardner once described to me a summer-camp snipe hunt in which he participated—I can't remember if it was as joker or jokee—in which the jokers enlisted the local police to arrive with lights flashing and sirens wailing at the peak of the hunt to arrest the entire group of campers for snipe hunting without licenses.

I now hunt woodcock instead of snipe. The two birds—who are cousins—migrate through here at about the same time, so I have to choose one or the other. Sam, like many dogs, points woodcock, but not snipe. Then there's Pam, who prizes woodcock above all other game (as I'm leaving to hunt deer or pheasant she says: "Wear plenty of orange" and "Don't let anyone shoot you." But on woodcock days it's: "Don't give any birds away."). So the snipe have been getting off easy in recent years, and I spend as many of my October afternoons as possible in the hills of northeast Iowa looking for woodcock.

And yes, I have eaten them innards intact in the French manner, which is not bad—the *entrailles* reminded me of cooked oysters—but I draw the line at leaving the heads on.

What we usually do with woodcock is split them and stick them under the broiler for a while, about six minutes a side.

If you want to try them with the *entrailles* left in, do this:

Rub nutmeg and butter on your plucked, undrawn birds. Put them in a baking dish and pour three tablespoons of cream on each. Cook the birds in a medium oven—375ish— for twenty-five minutes or so. Salt and pepper to taste. Serve on sourdough toast.

· · ·

The other appeal of woodcock hunting is the possibility of grouse, which can be chased in the same northeast Iowa coverts where the woodcock alight during migration.

I cannot figure grouse out well enough to hunt them effectively, but I suspect the reason they're hard to understand is that they don't have any idea what they're doing themselves. This brings me to an embarrassing story, which I will tell here as quickly as possible: Tom Culp and I, with no dog, are beating through the brush above North Cedar Creek, walking forty yards apart. There's a whir of wings at Tom's feet and a gray blur, barely glimpsed through foliage by me. Tom shoots. The blur is now visible as a grouse, coming my way. The grouse lands on a log ten feet from me, walks back and forth, regarding me blankly. Me, not wanting to shoot the grouse off a log, thinking: "This grouse must be hit or it wouldn't be acting so stupid. Better put him out of his misery." Reluctantly, but sure that I'm doing the right thing, I head-shoot the grouse where he stands. Holding up the bird for Tom to see, I say: "It's okay, Tom. I got your cripple." Tom then holds up a dead grouse himself. "What cripple?" he calls back. "I was shooting at this one."

Like the dove, the woodcock and the grouse, I believe, were not legal birds in Iowa in your day, although their illegality had nothing to do with any scriptural reference to grouse and woodcock, of which I am certain there are none. True?

> Love,
> Philip

.   .   .

> Baton Rouge, LA

Dear Philip,

You're right. No legal grouse and woodcock for me while I lived in Iowa. I did get to go after them for one wonderful week in Wisconsin and wrote about it in a piece called "Something New for the Old Gun," which is in my out-of-print, alas, *Country Matters*, and among the hunting pieces of mine I like best. It was one of those that flowed so nicely from my fingers through the keyboard and onto the paper that I actually had a good time writing it.

But, since we seem to be doing miscellaneous birds, let me move on to quail, bobwhite and desert.

Bobwhites were always legal in Iowa, and the hunting for them pretty good a half day's drive away, down along the Iowa-Missouri border. But my most memorable, if puzzling quail hunt, was one of those ducal, deep southern affairs of which I first learned from a newspaper photograph. It was of Charles Wilson, who had been president of General Motors and became Eisenhower's Secretary of Defense. He was riding in a mule-drawn wagon, sitting beside the driver, and the wagon appeared to have dozens of quail piled up behind the hunters.

Your mother and I were invited to join one such hunt in

Mississippi by Charles *"Pumping Iron"* Gaines, old friend and student, and the closest thing the field sports have to Arnold Schwarzenegger. In fact, I think by writing the book, Charles invented Arnold. Once when I was trout fishing in Wisconsin with Charles and Dick Wentz, another good writer, Gaines picked me up and carried me through strong current to get back from a sandbar we'd been fishing from. Didn't seem to be much effort for him, either.

Charles's stepfather was an important Birmingham industrialist, and he belonged to a club that leased several thousand acres of prime quail range over in Mississippi. I suspect the kind of hunt we experienced must have gone on in the South during plantation days, and must be the closest equivalent we have to the kind of estate hunting that goes on, if it still does, among the British nobility.

To begin with, we were all mounted, though I suppose a nonhorseman could have climbed up on the wagon seat like Sec. Wilson.

There were two wagons that day, pulled by mule teams, and containing dogs in individual pens—one wagon for the pointers, the other for the retrievers. Each wagon had a driver, of course, and in addition to the four of us was a man-in-charge. I don't feel "guide" is a lofty enough title for him.

We rode from one field to another. They'd been selected by the man-in-charge on the basis of reports from fellows who'd been sent out at daybreak, listening for bobwhites to give each other wake-up calls, as they do. Reaching a particular field, we'd dismount. The wagon drivers would hand us our shotguns and then get down to hold the horses. Then the man-in-charge would decide which trio of pointing dogs to release this time, and off they'd run, quartering the field. If one found birds and pointed, the other two were trained to back him, going on point as well.

The man-in-charge—maybe I should call him the master of bird hounds—would signal to us.

It was all pretty unhurried. We'd stroll over, load and set

up, and the master would walk in and flush the covey. This, I should say, is what was supposed to happen. We were then to shoot at the covey rise, call off the pointers, and let loose several of the retrievers to find the downed birds.

But on our day, the man-in-charge, as I'll go back to calling him, was mystified. He was getting a lot of false points. The dogs weren't at all eager to work. He was getting wild flushes, too, as well as coveys that wouldn't flush. We did get a few. We even spent time hunting singles, which was unusual—generally the hunt moves on after a covey rise.

The horses were bad, too, alternately skittish and sluggish, and quite determined to get out of there and head for home. The mules felt the same way.

Then the sky turned spooky green, it got very still, and the man-in-charge said, "Oh, boy. I did hear a tornado warning this morning, but it wasn't supposed to be coming this way."

We headed back, and learned when we got in that the tornadoes had touched down in several places within twenty miles of us. The birds, horses, dogs, and mules all seemed to have known it was a time to take cover, we guessed because of strange barometric pressures.

I wouldn't mind trying one of those high-style hunts again; they still go on. I read the other day that one of our senators had been invited on one by an appropriately located governor. At the same time, I'd equally enjoy being out again with Dave Wilson and Johnny Brenner, slogging up and down through sand and cactus in the hot, Arizona desert around Tucson.

It was exhausting, and no place for dogs. But you could locate desert quail by calling—unlike bobwhites in the day-time, they'd call back. In fact, sometimes you'd hear them (John and Dave would, anyway) without using the call at all.

Beautiful birds, with plumed heads.

I've one more quail anecdote I think deserves to be written down. One fall Ralph Ellison was teaching in Chicago and asked me if I could keep his black Labrador, a huge, friendly animal named Tuck, for him. We were then living in North Liberty, Iowa, and Ralph could get down there to visit Tuck from time to time. He was a good duck dog, as I recall it, but a little too boisterous for upland birds.

Pheasants opened on Saturday. Ralph came along to join me and Moon in the field on Sunday, and we hunted along, chatting, shooting, hitting or missing pheasants and rabbits. It seemed to me that Ralph's shooting was very like mine— *random* might be the word, but with occasional success.

We came to a small grove of trees, with a little open grass cover beside it; Moon ran into the cover and locked on point. Ralph and I followed in, walked around the dog, expecting another pheasant. Two surprising things happened almost simultaneously. A covey of quail flushed, and Ralph's gun fired twice before I even had mine to my shoulder; three birds fell.

"Hey," I said, "that's not the way you've been shooting."

Ralph smiled. "The first hunting I did was when I was a young boy near Detroit. I used to go out with an old, black, market hunter. I'd have a single shot, and sometimes no more than two or three shells, which cost a nickel each. Mostly we shot rabbits and sold them for ten cents each to the black families. Ten cents was a lot of money in the Depression. But every now and then we'd raise a covey of quail, and those were worth fifty cents a bird when we'd take them to the white suburb where the motor-car executives lived . . ."

I won't guarantee that those were his very words, but that's the substance of what he told me, and certainly needed no further explanation. But it makes a pretty striking contrast with the Deep South kind of hunt I opened with.

Love,
Dad

Chapter 10

THE SLUMP

From a postcard showing a rooster pheasant standing in a grassy field, "Iowa" written in red letters in one corner:

Dear Dad,

Pheasant season opens Saturday and I'll be at work, as always. Shaun and I do plan to get out Sunday morning. Looks like lots of birds around. Most corn is picked. Should be a great year. Wish you were here.

Philip

. . .

Baton Rouge, LA

Dear Philip,

Off he goes, into the somewhat tame blue yonder, cackling like a scolding mother. The tail flows out, maybe fatally for him, because by this we know, as well as by the cackle (which some genetically improved pheasants omit) that he is cock, not hen. So pheasant season opens with, of course, a bang.

The question is, I guess, when you contributed your initial bang, day before yesterday, was it followed by Sam's leaping to retrieve—or did he, as Moondog used to do when I missed, give you a reproachful, totally unsympathetic look?

When a season opens, it's nice to get the first one.

And pheasants were always my favorite opening—not because I always got the first one, as most surely I did not, and not because the birds themselves were really my first-choice targets. No, it was because when pheasants finally opened, everything was open—ducks, geese, quail, snipe, doves across the border in Illinois, and by now you have grouse and woodcock, too. I remember the wonderful feeling that as long as there was enough daylight to shoot by, I could legally do so at any bird on the list. Squirrels and rabbits, too.

Wish I was there, I sure do. My favorite weather. November in the Midwest. Golden weather.

Love,
Dad

. . .

Homestead, IA

Dear Dad,

What is Sam, to quote Shakespeare on dogs, but a tail wagged by an idiot? Hit or miss, he runs in high-strung circles when a pheasant gets up. On Sunday morning he got plenty of exercise. Half the birds cackled, half did not. Some cacklers lived and some silent birds died, so the process of natural selection by shotgun followed no discernible pattern.

The first bird was not long-tailed and cackling but a bird of the year, still working on his grown-up feathers. He ran out of the grass at the edge of the bean field where we started the season. Thinking it would be a bad omen to ground-swat the first pheasant of the year, I waited till he flew, then missed with both barrels. Missed two more after that, wing-tipped my first bird a little later on—the dogs got him—and finally centered one a few minutes later.

Not a brilliant showing to be sure. On the other hand, why do I assume, as so many people do, that I can take a gun out of the cabinet after a ten-month layoff and shoot it well?

Love,
Philip

. . .

Dear Philip,

If missing pheasants is the result of being out of practice, then kindly (or unkindly if necessary) explain the following recollection.

I've pondered this one off and on for the past twenty-five years, and it's going to take a page or two to set it forth for you to ponder, if you care to.

It begins with Lou Black, who was then as far into his sixties as I was into my forties—couple of years. Lou had been the banjo player for the New Orleans Rhythm Kings, the first great white jazz band out of Chicago. He'd also played pro football on weekend afternoons, though I can't tell you exactly at what level, and in spite of the Illinois location, I don't believe he was out there tackling Red Grange, or Jim Thorpe, or even Bronco Nagurski.

He was big enough, but probably too sweet-natured to have competed that hard.

What he did compete at was trapshooting. After he left music and football, both of which died economically during the Depression, he worked as a brick salesman in Rock Island, and two or three times a year friends would back him as a contestant in national trapshoots. Big old bald, smiling Lou Black and the friends won a lot of money that way, in purses and bets.

The eye-hand coordination that made him a fine musician, the strength and endurance that made him a successful athlete—these and a nice, relaxed self-confidence, along with the pure pleasure he took in the field sports—must account for Lou's having been the best shot and best tackle handler I've ever known.

It's not part of the ponder, but worth noting (footnoting?) that Lou survived the other members of the Rhythm Kings—George Brunis, Leon Rappolo, Emmet Hardy, and the rest—because he was diabetic and couldn't drink.

One late August afternoon back in the sixties I visited Lou to talk about where we might open the Illinois dove season. Now I'm a guy, as you well know, who cannot shoot clay, but that afternoon, with Lou standing right behind me, I really powdered some birds. His eyesight was so good he could see the shot patterns forming in the air in front of us. "You're shooting under them," he said. "Block them out. Squeeze off when you can't see 'em."

I don't know if that's the right shooting advice for everyman, but it worked for me that day. The good shooting carried over into the dove opening. I was behind a wooden fence that surrounded a barnyard with a stock tank in it full of water, and the birds were either coming into the water or flying by it to have a look at what the thirsty doves were up to.

I got my twelve-dove limit with seventeen shells. Unheard of. Just couldn't miss. I limited out before Lou himself did, an act of 12-gauge lèse-majesté.

And this spectacular shooting carried on through several more dove hunts, and then into the teal season, when bluewings fell for me as never before. I hit snipe. I hit quail. I was ready for pheasant opening, fellers, and I hardly need tell you how that one turned out: I had five shots at cocks Opening Day and missed them all.

Had an old duck hunter acquaintance who scorned pheasants. "Like shooting kites," he used to say, and there I was, a man who couldn't hit a kite.

The bad shooting carried over just as the good shooting had. I could miss rabbits. I could miss squirrels. And I continued to avoid doing any damage to the pheasants; even the surprise factor couldn't be blamed, since Moon was working well, holding birds and cursing me in dogthought when I missed. The only thing that stopped me from buying a kite, tying on a pheasant tail-feather, and using it to practice on was the problem of whom I might find to fly it for me. Low.

Love,
Dad

. . .

Homestead, IA

Dear Dad,

My rooster-shooting woes continue.

The problem with pheasants, I've decided, is that there's no apparent reason to miss them. Grouse and woodcock are forever putting branches between you and them. Doves, we all know, twist and turn unpredictably, and besides, everyone misses doves. If you miss, say, a grouse, you think, Well, there was a branch in my eye; I'll get the next one. You're relaxed, and you shoot well. Miss a pheasant and you think, How could I have missed such a big, slow, easy target? A few such inexplicable misses in a row and self-doubt begins to erode your confidence. I can remember going out with Vern Zach, who is, as you know, deadly, on a day when he missed five or six roosters and hit none. We ended the afternoon standing on the bridge over Old Man's Creek, with Vern mumbling to himself and shooting at snags in the water to see if he'd forgotten to put shot in his reloads.

My theory would explain your outshooting Lou Black on doves then missing five roosters on Opening Day. It would also explain what happened to me yesterday.

I had missed, before yesterday morning, six roosters in a row. I then missed number seven around nine o'clock. As I wound up to throw my gun in the creek, Cousin Shaun diplomatically suggested we take a break from pheasants and look up some woodcock in the willow thickets.

The migrants were in; Alex (Shaun's dog) was handling them nicely, grinding to a halt in his slow, steady way as he scented birds. Shaun let me have the first crack at all the birds we saw. I killed four with five shots as they twisted through the trees. No one ever called woodcock "kites," either.

"I really think I can hit a pheasant now," I said hopefully, whereupon I missed a gimme shot at a rooster not long after we returned to the cornfields.

Love,
Philip

. . .

Baton Rouge, LA

Dear Philip:

A shooting slump—I hope you're not in one. Me, I went from being a .400 hitter in the early season to maybe .027 by play-off time. I guess it's like a baseball player's hitting slump. People give you good advice: *Change your stance. You may be left-eyed: try closing it.* And even, as one friend said, not knowing he was echoing Lou Black, "Block it out. You may be shooting underneath."

I remember hunting one day along the creek on the far side, through some nice grass, with visions of paté in my mind. Moon and I were clearly trailing birds, and I feared they'd flush wild and distant, but instead they stopped when the grass ran out at a place along the creek bank. So they were squatting on the edge of the creek when we came up; they flushed in easy range, four of them, going straight out across the creek like jumped ducks. I picked a bird, thinking I might get a double. I fired three times. I missed three times.

"That paté's not quite ready for the oven," said Pete Neill, who was hunting with me.

"I was shooting with my left eye closed," I explained. "Next shot I'm going to close the right one, too."

Love,
Dad

. . .

Homestead, IA

Dear Dad,

Before, I thought it was just bad shooting. But your fears, and mine, are realized: This is an all-out, debilitating, confidence-destroying slump. I've missed thirteen in a row since I hit that last bird on the opener, and I'm afraid to shoot at more for fear of missing them and adding to my string.

Your exchange with Pete Neal recalls the one I had with Tom Culp the other day. The corn was being picked on either side of the neighbor's farm, and birds were flushing ahead of the combines in the corn and landing in the big field we were hunting. I haven't seen so many birds in years. Sam kept pointing them dutifully. I missed and missed and missed. Three times Tom let me start shooting, waited until my gun was empty, then dropped the bird. Finally I said: "Let's go back to the car for more bullets. I've only got five left, and I'm saving the last one for myself."

"Save two," said Tom. "You'll probably miss."

I don't know how much longer I can stand this.

Love,
Philip

. . .

Baton Rouge, LA

Dear Philip:

Knowing all too well the near-terminal despair of the pheasant-slumper, I dropped everything yesterday and sped to New Orleans to the voodoo shop to get you a slump-curing mojo. They had them for goose and duck, quail, woodcock and dove, but none for pheasants.

Not a Louisiana bird, they said, implying that if it were not a Louisiana bird, it hardly mattered whether one hit or missed it.

After further thought they did say that if you could send them the gizzard stones from an albino pheasant, shot by starlight on a moonless night, along with the blood of a pheasant-eating bull snake and a fifty-dollar deposit, they could probably get the conjure people to fix something up, but couldn't guarantee it.

I said I'd be right back with the stuff, but forgot to ask whether you were to take it orally or smear it on your gun.

While we wait, maybe a biblical injunction will do the trick: Pheasants thou must kill, my son. Thou hast a woman and child at home weary with eating dried cuttlefish and buckwheat groats.

Let me know if it works.

Love,
Dad

. . .

Homestead, IA

Dear Dad:

My slump is over: This week I've killed five birds with as many shells. It's a little too soon to look back at the last couple of weeks and laugh, but I'm ready to enjoy pheasant hunting again and I'll take my misses in stride when they come.

Now that I am hitting again, I've been trying to figure out if there is anything to be learned about shooting from my slump and subsequent recovery. I'm not sure there is, but I've noticed something I'd already been semi-aware of: on the days when I can hit, I'm possessed of a confidence that borders on prescience. Those days, I know long before the flush that I'm going to hit whatever I shoot at. This is not a state of mind I can summon at will. Good shooters probably can.

It was Monday, finally, when my confidence returned. I'd taken Sam over to my landlord's farm to hunt his fence lines. Since the cover was sparse, I didn't bother to put the bell on the dog's collar, so when he disappeared around a corner post there was no reason for me to know he was stopped and on point around the bend. But all of a sudden I knew he was, just as surely as I knew he was pointing a rooster, not a hen, and that there was no way in the world I would miss this shot.

Nor did I. I had a strange, déjà vu feeling that the whole thing was already decided, that all I had to do was walk around the corner and shoot the bird. I felt as if I were stepping into those numbered footprints you see in ballroom-dance manuals as I walked up to Sam. Kicking the bird out from under Sam's nose and watching him fly away, I found myself wondering how anyone could ever miss anything with a shotgun. When he'd got far enough out to let the pattern open up sufficiently, I dropped him into the black furrows of the cornfield.

I haven't missed a bird since. Maybe it's the Cajun mojo working. More likely, I think my subconscious knew that the law of averages would catch up with me eventually and I finally relaxed. Whatever the case, the local pheasants are now in serious trouble, and the dried cuttlefish can breathe a long sigh of relief.

Love,
Philip

Chapter 11

CRITTERS

Baton Rouge, LA

Dear Philip,

Friend called me up this morning to offer me a chance to go squirrel hunting. It was not to be with him—it was a hunt he'd arranged for and couldn't make—so I had no trouble declining. But it wasn't just because I tend to be a bird snob. Of the furred small-game animals, squirrels were my favorite in Iowa days; as with other things, there was an idiosyncratic way of taking them that appealed to me. (I don't know if I ever mentioned that my favorite way of duck hunting was floating the river in a canoe, one guy paddling, gunner up-front, on a nice fall day; the ducks would jump as we appeared from around a bend or went past a sand bar. This is oddly parallel to what I settled on in the squirrel department.)

To go back, the reason I don't hunt squirrels in Louisiana is laziness. The usual squirrel down here is not the big, red, Brunswick stew fox-squirrel, but the small gray one, which doesn't look worth the considerable task of skinning and dressing to me. There is also the southern flying squirrel, but before you suggest the possibility of wing-shooting, I'd better say that these guys are the size of a chipmunk.

In addition, to some extent squirrel hunting depends on decent hearing, not the strongest of my five declining senses.

A waverer is what I was at the outset as to weapon and method. One friend and mentor scorned the shotgun: "Squirrel hunting is a rifleman's sport," he said. "And the .22 is perfect—enough range, enough bullet size, and a challenge to a guy's skill." Having more rifle than shotgun vanity, I'd go for the rifle challenge.

"I won't use a rifle on them," said another, a good shot, too. "I've seen too many gut-shot squirrels disappear into holes in trees, to die up there. I want that 12-gauge impact that kills them right now, with enough shock so that they come down from the branch. Straight down. *Thump.*" And I'd find myself agreeing that *thump* was the sound I wanted to try to hear.

Did you know there was a frontiersman's compromise? It was—maybe still is—called "barking," and it was done with a rifle. You aimed at the spot on the tree branch just under the squirrel's chin. The wood chip in the throat was what did the critter in, but I think something larger than a .22 bullet must have been involved; the point was to avoid making a big hole and messing up the meat.

My shotgun man was devoted to calling, which, like all game calling, can be interesting. Calling does bring out the squirrels, of course, but the squirrel called forth by that territorial chattering is apt to be pretty active. Seems best to go for the *thump.*

My .22-toting friend, a real purist, is the one whose method I adopted, suiting it to the hilly woods on the farm. It was a variety of stalking, for which I'd wear moccasins when I could, because it involved stepping slowly and silently up one side of a small hill, occasionally leaning down to remove a dry leaf here, a twig there. Just before the crest I'd get down on my knees, then my stomach for the last foot or two, so that I could peer down the reverse hillside unseen. If I'd been really quiet, there might well be a squirrel or two, messing around on the ground with fallen acorns or hickory nuts. From a prone position. For the head. If you miss, no gut-shot squirrel.

Love,
Dad

. . .

Homestead, IA

Dear Dad,

Squirrel hunting, I'll agree, presents more options as to method and weapon than do most kinds of hunting, and I've tried several of them. So not only do I know what barking is, I've done it, thank you very much, although I guess what I did was "dirt clodding," since the squirrel was on the ground, not up a tree at the time. The proper rifle for barking, as you correctly surmise, is rather larger than a .22 rimfire. In my case it was a 50-caliber muzzleloader, although I believe D. Boone and friends preferred 36-caliber rifles for squirrels. My muzzleloader was a rifle I acquired with deer hunting in mind but foolishly sold after a year or two. I did squirrel hunt with it some, and did once shoot under a squirrel's chin; the resulting concussion killed him stone dead, leaving no mark other than a bloody nose.

The muzzleloader was the third of four arms I've experimented with during my intermittent squirreling, the first having been the .410, which is not a bad squirrel gun. The crash-thump of a squirrel coming down through the branches notwithstanding, I moved on to the .22, in concert with a call or my own method of stalking—spotting a squirrel in a tree and easing close enough to rest the gun on the trunk and shoot straight up. The problem here (and with the .22's briefly adopted replacement, the muzzleloader) is the idea of that bullet, having traveled high into the air, falling to earth like a satellite whose orbit has decayed, screaming down to thump into someone's windshield or cow.

This is a populous state, after all, by rural standards. The chance was about the same as that of the windshield or cow being hit by Skylab, but the thought of it happening always lurked in the back of my mind.

What I've settled on, eccentrically enough, is an air rifle, an extremely accurate German-made Beeman 177-caliber rifle, topped with an equally German 2 × 7 variable scope. The light pellet poses less danger on reentry than does a .22 bullet—not to mention a 50-caliber round-ball—but it will kill squirrels very dead at modest ranges. These pellets are deadly, but they must be placed precisely in order to kill. They're so light that you really need a windless day to squirrel hunt with an air gun, and we have precious few of those in Iowa in the fall. My squirrel-hunting opportunities, therefore, are severely limited by my choice of weapon.

Indoors, in the winter, I use the air gun somewhat reluctantly to shoot any mouse who proves too clever for our traps. Mouse shooting is not my favorite thing to do as there are no good mouse recipes I know about (maybe in a Cajun cookbook?), and the pelts are too small to make anything out of.

Which reminds me of something my landlord told me the other day. He used to run a trap line for skunks back in the 'teens when you could still sell skunk pelts. He checked his traps on the way to the one-room country schoolhouse each morning. If he had good luck and caught several skunks, he tells me, not only would he make a little money, but he would smell so bad when he got to school that the teacher would send him home for the day.

So, having steered the topic to pelts, let me finally ask you a question I've never asked: I still have the coonskin cap you had made for me at Mitvalsky's with the one coon you ever shot. I remember distinctly wearing that hat to school when it was nothing more than a sewn-up hide with salt and pieces of raccoon meat stuck on the inside. I must have been in the second or third grade. Why on earth did you let me go to school wearing a rotting raccoon skin on my head?

Love,
Philip

. . .

Baton Rouge, LA

Dear Philip,

Your coonskin hat recollection is far more vivid than mine, but I do remember that I shot the animal in broad daylight with your uncovered head primarily in mind. The secondary motive—and let me interpolate that I never shot another coon except for a scrawny one that was laying waste to our ducks and chickens—had to do with a regular Friday-night poker game that I mentioned earlier in this correspondence.

Your cap-coon was out on a tree limb, watching me and Moondog hunt pheasants. He was a magnificent, winter-coated creature, and very large. He gave me time to change my pheasant loads to number fours, and I dropped him with the fine *thump* likewise mentioned above. Moon wasn't sure whether to retrieve him or not, and I settled the matter by removing the dead coon from the tentative jaws of dog, and carried coon to the car by the tail.

Skinned him at home, salted him, with Mitvalsky's skill at turning fur into garments my goal, whenever time permitted a run to Cedar Rapids. And now I'm going to say that it must have been you who couldn't wait for tanning, lining, and transformation. I think you wanted to wear that raw skin to school. So I must have stitched it up crudely for you. Oh, well. I'm pleased you still have the Mitvalsky creation, knowing that Chipper's head will grow to fit it in good time.

The coon meat was cut into serving pieces and barbecued. My vanity required that each Friday at 11:30 we take a break from our intense rounds of dealer's choice, and that I serve something, generally game, to the players, five or six hungry graduate students. The barbecued coon was a real success, though not as unforgettable as the possum potpies made a week or two earlier from the only possum I ever dispatched. Had to. He was playing dead, as they do, and this time Moon was determined to retrieve; I didn't want that possum to rise from the dead and go for Moondog's throat, so I held dog off with one hand and did shotgun coup de grace with the other.

But with coons and possums, as with squirrels and rabbits, I never became inflamed with the kind of hunting passion roused by upland birds and waterfowl. I was thinking about this the day before yesterday, as I pondered what to say in this letter while watching four squirrels play some mad game, up and down a smallish tree in my backyard. It was a chasing game, fast, funny, and sweet, and I had no inclination at all to interrupt their revels with slaughter and consumption.

Instead I found myself reminded of a conversation I had with a friend we'd made a year or so ago in Paris. She was an Australian traveler named Helen, who liked to eat as well as any other tourist drawn to Paris by the food. One day I remarked to Helen that I'd heard kangaroo meat was delicious, maybe the best eating provided by any of those outback wild creatures.

Helen said she'd heard the same thing.

"But have you never tried it?"

"Would you eat your pet?" Helen asked.

It struck a chord in Paris that didn't actually sound until day before yesterday in Louisiana. Those smaller animals of the woods and fields, when you've spent a lot of time outdoors as you and I have, do become almost petlike, collectively.

They have another quality that gives them anthropomorphic protection from me. I identify with their rage to survive, and with the speed, cunning, and sometimes courage with which they express it. Not long after I'd struck down the coon, Moon, the protagonist of so much of this entry, and I were once again after pheasants out near the reservoir, when he chased up a mink.

I'd never seen one alive before, a tiny creature really, long and thin, and absolutely dauntless, weighing probably less than two pounds. Moon was between him and whatever den he wanted to reach, and apparently Moon regarded the mink as something like a long, thin, tiny cat. The idea would be, then, to get a dog's jaw in position to grab this thing by the back, give it a shake, and break it.

Moon weighed a good fifty pounds and was in excellent fighting trim. That mink fought off our tough old weimaraner for five furious minutes. It fought on its hind legs, whirling to keep its back covered, and biting Moon on the nose, which would make the dog yell and back off, only to charge again with a bleeding nose. There were rounds in which the mink was the aggressor, and it finally backed Moon off far enough to give it a clear line to the den, for which it raced with amazing speed.

I could have shot it. I didn't want to. Otherwise, you might have had a single, wild mink earmuff to wear to school.

Love,
Dad

. . .

Homestead, IA

Dear Dad,

I see. And I suppose if I'd announced that I couldn't wait until I turned sixteen to drive myself to school you'd have said, "Sure, go ahead, take the car. You're in the third grade. You know what's best for you." You could have stopped me from wearing that hat, you know.

Ultimately, I have to agree with you on the subject of critters. When I hunt deer and turkeys I rely on the coons, possums, and squirrels to keep me entertained during the long vigils in the woods. They are too amusing to watch, by and large, for serious shooting and eating or skinning and garment-making.

My reluctance to kill critters explains the mannered and

inefficient approach I've adopted for small-game hunting—
air guns at ten paces—and the importance both you and I
seem to attach to the method of hunting.

Rabbits would be quite another matter—easy to skin,
delicious, they exude a continuous hyperawareness of the
fact that they are very good to eat, which makes them a little
easier to kill than clownish squirrels.

Unfortunately, I can't shoot rabbits over Sam, since I have
problems enough with his chasing birds and airplanes without encouraging him to race after ground game, too.

The answer (my answer, anyway) would be to buy about
ten beagles—enough so I could lose one or two for a few
days at a time and not really notice—and hunt rabbits full-
time from the end of pheasant season in early January to the
end of rabbit season, February 28. I've tried to explain to Pam
that ten beagles wouldn't really be like having ten dogs,
because a dog pack has a sort of single, group brain. Think of
them, I say, as one giant dog with forty feet. Curiously, this
argument fails to persuade.

This is perhaps just as well, because while rabbits remain
high on my seemingly ever-shrinking list of shootable critters, Chipper, at age three, has adopted them as his totem
animal. He carries his stuffed bunny to bed. His Halloween
costume consisted of long ears, whiskers, and a cotton tail.
He adores our car, a Volkswagen Rabbit. Bunnies, he tells me,
say "Dee, dee, dee"—this may well be true, at least at the
high frequencies audible only to dogs, rabbits, and children.

If I brought home dead rabbits, he'd want to play with
them, and I'm not sure I could stand it.

I'm reminded that you wrote about me in *The Unnatural
Enemy*, when I was just a little older than Chipper, that I was
still too much of a squirrel, a rabbit, or a winged bird myself
for you to want me to see you killing them. I now know
exactly how you felt, but I realize there's another side of it,
too. Children are as much hawks, owls, and coyotes as they
are rabbits, squirrels, and birds; if not, we would never grow

up to be hunters. The fierce, uncomplicated pleasure children can take in predation—not that much different from a
bird dog's love of the hunt—is a reminder that hunting your
own dinner is a perfectly natural thing to do and enjoy. We're
the ones who are too old and encumbered by guilt to remember that sometimes. Chipper is already insisting that we go
fishing and bring the fish home and eat them for dinner.
When I try to explain that we might put the little ones back
to grow bigger, or that sometimes we don't keep any fish at
all, he gets quite upset.

I guess that's part of what you called the "C'mon, Dad"
factor in an earlier letter thanking me for pushing you back
into the field again after you thought you'd left for good. I'm
glad I could do it for you, even if it took a few extra years, and
I hope, if and when the time comes, Chipper will do the same
for me.

Love,
Philip

PART THREE

Fungus, Books, and Alligators

When Philip got big enough to use a chainsaw and splitting maul, he and I used to work in the woods together. A previous owner of what became Redbird Farm had sold the fine stand of white oak in the largest of the timber areas to a barrel man.

The barrel man uses white oak to make the barrels in which whiskey is aged. It's a wasteful kind of harvesting because only the first four feet at the butt of the tree are used to make staves. The rest of the trunks and tops were scattered sadly through the woods when we bought the farm, though when freshly cut they could have been made into lumber. People don't like to build with white oak. It's very tough; you bend a lot of nails trying to hammer into it, even when it's fresh, and the trunks I'm speaking of had become seasoned and extra hard.

That made them wonderful for firewood. Green white-oak is so dense you can hardly get it to burn, but the seasoned wood, once lit, will burn a long, long time.

Every September I would build a white-oak fire in the schoolhouse fireplace and keep it going until spring, making sure it smoldered all night, feeding it until it flamed in the chill of the mornings.

So, during the summers, if I'd got caught up with the garden work, Philip and I would go out and make firewood, to stack outdoors along the south side of the schoolhouse till there was enough to last all winter. That would be a pile about twenty feet long and as high as my head.

When the pile was done, we'd sell truckloads of firewood to people in town, too, sometimes Philip and I, sometimes Philip and his friend Matt Culp, whose brother Tom accompanied Philip on a pheasant hunt during the infamous slump.

You have to keep the chain on your saw very sharp to handle white oak, and the grain is so dense that you often can't split a log with the maul alone but have to use a wedge or two as well. It was hot, sweaty, and glorious, out there in the timber, with our shirts off, sawdust tickling our forearms, and the sharp smell of tannin and the soft one of leaf mold. Splitting wood, and especially difficult wood, was a kind of physical labor I always enjoyed. Hickory, ash, and red oak were fun in a different way: you could often split a log with a single stroke of the maul, which is gratifying, but not like the problem-solving of where to put the wedge and how to angle it when you're working up white oak.

Then Philip would go off, back to his school in Spain, or, later on, to college, and I'd start hunting. I guess I've brought up working in the woods to let you know about one of the things we liked to do that doesn't come up in the letters.

During those years, I collected a fair number of books about hunting and fishing. They stayed on the farm when I left, and Philip has them now. We write about some of them in the section that follows, and then about something else I did a lot of when the seasons came, which was hunting mushrooms. I've done just a little of it in Louisiana, but I'm not familiar with the places and the local varieties, so that getting into the car and trying to find a location is nothing like the pleasure I used to take in following the impulse to take a stroll with my basket, going through those hills and draws in which so many of my hours were spent and of which I never got tired. There were always new things there.

In the early spring, waiting for the first mushrooms, I used to photograph the first wildflowers. I had a Nikon with a macro lens, which made for great close-ups. I remember one of a trillium blossom with an ant on one of the petals, and a drop of dew. Philip's sister Robin has the outfit now and uses it very well. One year she made me a calendar for Christmas, with an appropriate one of her photographs to illustrate each month. The days and dates no longer match, of course, but I keep the calendar for the pictures.

Of the people appearing in Part III only one, being someone Philip met when he was down here, needs to be identified for the reader. She is Jon Kemp, who was my administrative assistant at LSU one year. She's Southern in the nicest way, full of energy and high spirits (though Jon can get into the damnedest depressions, too, out of which I was generally able to cajole her). Her duties included, along with PR and scheduling, at both of which she was a whiz, making sure I turned off the electric typewriter before I left the office. She was very stern about it.

The lectures in India mentioned in the final chapter were for the United States Information Service and took place at the American Studies Research Center in Hyderabad, where the Indian scholars wanted to hear about the American experience of the Second World War. What the USIS had to find was a survivor. They're getting scarce.

Chapter 12

FUNGUS

Baton Rouge, LA

Dear Philip:

You have an absolutely first-class sister. Know what she did? For my birthday last fall she sent me a one-quart mason jar full of dried morel mushrooms, harvested, I assume, by her own dainty hands.

There were 39 of the beauties, packed up with four bay leaves and a spoonful of peppercorns. Some of the morels were no bigger than my thumbnail—they shrink, of course, in drying but pretty much double in size when soaked preparatory to cooking; some were as big as my thumb, and all were hoarded through the winter months like jewels (or rather, unlike jewels, unless we count Cleopatra's reputed taste for drinking pearls dissolved in wine) and consumed in batches of three or four. On going to the mushroom shelf I would first consider dried Italian porcinis, Chinese blacks, and shiitakes before deciding that the dish I wanted to prepare deserved morels.

Having so decided, I'd open the sealed jar and sniff. Even now, seven months after my birthday, the fumes are practically intoxicating and may well provide nourishment. I think my nose gains an ounce every time.

And I am reminded by the smell, and no less by the sight of the morels, of what was probably the most memorable meal we had in France last summer, in a summer of memorable meals.

We were in the North, in the mountainous part of Alsace, where apparently morels had flourished, been picked and dried, a couple of months earlier. We stayed a night or two at a very small, maybe six-bedroom, hotel, where there were always more local people in the dining room at dinnertime than there were hotel guests. In fact, we may have been the only hotel guests.

Victor, the chef, a man reassuringly fat if not notably jolly, served veal for dinner, braised, I guess, which came with something like a light béchamel sauce in which he'd cooked reconstituted morels. Oh. Ah. Oh. I wanted more the next morning for breakfast, which was considered too outlandish a request for any waiter to listen to seriously. *Ici le croissant, monsieur.* Besides, there was none of last night's dinner left over. I suspect Victor had eaten up all that remained himself.

The French, I might note, are fungal xenophobes. When I claimed, in my sophomore C-minus French, that I had once regularly gathered morels on my farm in the Midwest, it was quite clear to them that they had another childish American braggart on their hands, at whose absurd claims a fellow could only raise his chin—in Victor's case about four chins— and roll his eyes at his friend the croissant pusher. As well try to tell them Yanks raise veal.

Let's leave France. Here in Louisiana, still hallucinating from sniffing Robin's magic-mushroom jar, I am back in Iowa, waiting for spring. It's early April. Bloodroot has appeared as the ground dries out in the woods, under the trees, which are thinking about leafing out. The Mayapple plants are showing, weeks away from blooming yet, and there are buds but not blossoms on the apple tree. I know I shan't find any, but

I'm going to start checking some of the places where the very earliest, the thumbnail-sized morels, grew last year. *Morchella angusticeps* is what I decided they were, but I'm a tentative taxonomist, in spite of all the mushroom books I've acquired, and the microscope for looking at spores.

It will still be a week before I find any *angusticeps*, if I do this year, and they'll probably not be in those same places and I'll find them accidentally. I will be literally thrilled if I do gather some, not just because the first taste of spring is now in my hand but because it's an omen. I know now that given normal luck with moisture and temperatures, the thumb-sized boys (*esculenta* and *deliciosa*—succulent and delicious) will start in about three weeks. By Mother's Day, the first Sunday in May, they will be so abundant that I'll invite all the writing students, staff, and their families out for the annual mushroom hunt.

Wish I could have got dumb old Victor over for it once. Wish I could get dumb old me up there for it right now.

Hey Victor, here's a plane ticket. You can leave the croissant guy at home, but don't forget the veal.

Love,
Dad

. . .

Homestead, IA

Dear Dad,

Nice of Robin to share mushrooms with you. I'd send some myself, but I'm not finding any this year because my sister beats me to them. Since Robin now lives on my old mushrooming haunts (and yours) while I have moved fifteen miles away, she enjoys considerable home-field advantage over me. Compound this with the fact that I am a fundamentally lazy mushroomer, returning only to the places where I've hunted for years, and that I showed each and every one of my favorite spots to Robin years ago when she was too young to be serious competition, and you see why I keep coming up empty-handed. I have three equally unappealing alternatives before me: Go without morels, buy them for $12.99 a pound at the grocery store, or rely on the kindness of others to keep me in fungus.

Fortunately, I haven't had to stoop to buying my mushrooms because Robin has so many she doesn't know what to do with them all. She gave me a good-sized batch last week and another big bunch a few days ago. In the past, I have always insisted that since *I* find the mushrooms we have to cook them my way, fried in beer batter. Pam pointed out (a little too enthusiastically, I thought) that since I had not found these mushrooms, nor any others this year, she would cook them. Here's what she did:

Melted ½ stick unsalted butter in a skillet on low to medium heat.

Added 1 pound mushrooms, cut in half or thinly sliced, and 1 clove minced garlic when butter foamed—cooked until liquid evaporated, then until the mushrooms turned light brown, about 10–15 minutes.

Softly scrambled eggs (in a double boiler), folded mushrooms into eggs, sprinkled with a little tarragon. Served w/crusty French bread.

Unbelievable.

Here's another one we tried:

Sauté mushrooms in garlic, butter, and some scallions. Add cream and sage. Reduce a bit. Crumble in blue cheese, serve on fettucine w/grated Parmesan or Romano.

Even better than the first.

My mushroom-cooking horizons, along with my waistline, have been seriously broadened by this experience, and beer batter may be relegated to panfish and squash blossoms from now on.

There is, by the way, another morel I've been seeing on the rare occasions I find anything in the woods other than stems, one which I don't remember finding in other years. This would be a giant morel. The ones I've seen are almost ten inches tall, are brown, and look like a pitted football on a stick when you see them in the woods. They don't make as good eating as do the others. Do you know the ones I'm talking about?

Love,
Philip

. . .

Baton Rouge, LA

Dear Philip,

Yes, I know the ones you're talking about pretty well. They are *Gyromitra brunnea*, of a family sometimes called false morels, or, by the Germans, *Lorchels* for some heavily playful Germanic reason. *Brunneas* are also incorrectly called Beefsteak Mushrooms by some (see below for mo'), and there's a close relative, *Gyromitra esculenta*, known to some as the Arkansas Morel. Many are those who have eaten both for years and are still alive, and as well as if they hadn't. However, some specimens, the books warn, may contain a good, unhealthy dose of some unpleasant stuff called helvelic acid, and this is not a good thing to eat. Therefore, as one of the world's great mushroom cowards, I used to find *gyros*, identify them, and throw them about as far as a football on a stick could be thrown.

All in all, I identified and dared eat twenty-six species of fungi in my time on the farm, a period of sixteen pretty nice years. What I learned is what the preface to most any mushroom-hunting guide will tell you—that there are hundreds of kinds of fungi, just as there are hundreds of other kinds of plants, from wildflowers to walnut trees. Among the plants are a few we call fruits and vegetables, a few more that are poisonous, some more so than others; but the huge majority of them we don't eat and aren't tempted to. Same with fungi: a few edibles, some better than others; a few poisonous, some more so than others; and, again, a huge majority to which, under the heading "edible," we would mark *n/a*.

Among the fungi I found, though not often, was the one correctly called Beefsteak (*Fistulina hepatica*). It grows on oaks, is red on top and pinkish underneath, and is quite juicy, with a beefy texture. I thought them okay, but not among my favorites, and here is an oddity for you: In Europe they take the spawn of these guys and implant it in logs, harvest the mushrooms, and then saw up the log for extra-fine lumber. The mycelium (sort of a cross between a cobweb and a root system, out of which mushrooms grow) goes into and all through the log, creating an interesting pattern of red lines when it's cross-sectioned. Cabinetmakers like it a lot. Why Wayne Yoder and I never tried it at his sawmill I don't know; it was the sort of nutty thing I was known to attempt around there.

Favorites? There were seven, but only one concerning which a tale springs to mind.

Pete and Mimi Neill were going to China, and I'd been reading, probably in a Chinese cookbook, about a rare and magnificent mushroom they called the Monkey's Head. Zealots made long, perhaps dangerous journeys to the area where it grew, and so, when Pete asked what I wanted from China, I said, "Bring me a Monkey's Head mushroom and you shall have half my kingdom and my daughter's hand in marriage."

Since Robin was about four and Pete very happy with Mimi, and since the Iowa State Bank and Trust Company owned most of my kingdom, I felt I was on safe ground. Anyway, Pete failed to bring me a Monkey's Head, but he did bring me a Chinese mushroom book with fine illustrations— color drawings—in it. And there was a Monkey's Head illustrated—white, softball-sized, and hairy looking. Yes, I'd seen pictures of it before; it was a coral hydnum. And I'd yearned to find one ("edible and choice" said the books) but never had—until, a couple of weeks after the book arrived, damned if I didn't squish through a marshy area and *bingo*. Only one I ever saw. The question is: What do I owe Pete?

Love,
Dad

· · ·

Homestead, IA

Dear Dad,

Now you tell me. Either I have a high tolerance for helvelic acid or these really are giant morels, because I've been frying these big guys up and eating them with no ill effect this spring.

I've read, and you might confirm or refute this as your experience warrants, that *any* mushroom, eaten in sufficient quantity, will make you slightly ill. I tend to believe this after my experience with The Enormous Puffball last fall. While grouse hunting in Delaware County in October, I found a truly large puffball, big enough so that I could have served *Mushroom Stuffed with Grouse* if I'd wanted to. Actually, I measured it with a tape so I wouldn't make up outrageous stories about it: It was 29" in circumference. I cut off a slice and sautéed it when I got home—delicious.

In the name of scientific inquiry or just plain gluttony (I now forget which), I decided to try an experiment: How long could one man live off a single mushroom, hacking off and frying a slab whenever he got hungry? The answer was about a day and a half; then my stomach turned queasy and I tossed the remaining two-thirds of the puffball outside for the skunks to find.

So, is it possible to eat yourself sick on even "edible and choice" mushrooms? I vote yes. Good way to go, though.

What you owe Pete Neill, by the way, is a picture of half your kingdom or half a picture of your kingdom, and fortunately, no more than two or three fingers from one of your daughter's mushroom-grabbing hands.

Love,
Philip

. . .

Baton Rouge, LA

Dear Philip,

Though I can't confirm your "overdose of edible and choice" theory from dinner-table experience, I may have experienced something similar from fungus-by-needle. This would be the nice, beneficial fungus from which penicillin is derived, to which, after four or five injections over a ten-year period, I became violently allergic for life. The only beneficiary, if I had a good big shot of p. by now, would be the manager of the local crematorium. No more giant puffballs for you.

For you, however, quite possibly, chanterelles, to which I will now give you a verbal treasure map. Keep it locked in your sea chest (lacking a hollow wooden leg to hide it in), where Robin cannot find it:

Leaving the schoolhouse pasture, following the woods trail, there stands, on the right, just before the picnic ground, a cluster of five (I think) very large, old, white oaks, unless they have been harvested for lumber since I was there. From the trunk (not stump, I hope) of the last in line, there is a V of grass and weeds and probably multiflora rose opening on both flanks of the oak and closing where the picnic ground's perimeter begins. In that V, in June, grow, in unfortunately safe dosage, *Cantharellus cibarius*, the golden chanterelle: *Pfifferling* of the Germans, *girolles* in France, *kantarellas* in Scandinavia, *lisichki* in Russia. World-class good. I once ate in a restaurant in Illinois called The Golden Chanterelle, rather wistfully, since there were pictures of it on the wall but none offered on the menu. Sort of like naming your joint The Peacock's Tongue, I guess.

The first of three times I found chanterelles, other than on the farm, was at a commercial campground in Bar Harbor, Maine, near the entrance to the laundry room. They were fully in view, bright as could be, and people were carrying their laundry baskets right past, even trampling some of the mushrooms. I put my basket down to protect them, and found a pillowcase.

It was really a big patch. I won't claim to have filled the pillowcase, but I probably picked about a pound. Some guy stopped to see what Crazy was doing and finally asked:

"Are those good to eat or something?"

I was close enough to finished with my harvest so that I answered: "In Germany, where they're more common, they still cost thirty bucks a pound. Want to try a few?"

Sane shook his head, and walked off, still shaking it.

And then, of all places, I found them in September at the other end of the country. We'd gone to celebrate my birthday at an antebellum plantation home, where we spent the night. When I came back in from jogging next morning and cut across the lawn, I spotted chanterelles under the live oaks, enough to fill the hand-warming pocket that goes across the front of a hooded sweatshirt. This time it was the owner of the place who wanted to know what Crazy was doing and got told the price of *Pfifferlings*. Antebellum walked away, knowing a big fib when he heard one.

The third time was in Paris last summer, in a vegetable stall in an open-air market. They had 'em there on sale for a couple of weeks, and we bought them every day if we were eating at home. It must have been a good crop year, up in the Alps, since they weren't more than twenty bucks a pound. A bargain in gold.

Oh, yes. The other favorites, along with the morels and Monkey's Heads: *Volvariella bombycina*, which is so rare it doesn't have a common name and is the most beautiful mushroom I know. And three with wonderful common names: Goat's Beards, Parasols, and Shaggy Manes, all there for you to hunt and me to dream on.

Love,
Dad

Chapter *13*

——

GATORS

Baton Rouge, LA

Dear Philip,

This evening, driving back from—what could be more Louisianan?—my first alligator hunt, and thinking of writing to you about it, I realized that the gator is not the only amphibious creature I've pursued in search of nourishment and excitement.

There've been three: in order of fearsomeness, the frog, the snapping turtle, and now, the gator.

Anyone with even a vestigial sense of climax would agree, it seems to me, that these creatures must be considered in that same order, so let us begin with the frog. (The same sequence applies in two other ways: the number of times I hunted each and my interest in each as food.)

Certainly I've spent more days and nights after *Ranidae* than either of the other pets and been a frog legs–please guy.

I remember my first frog, oddly enough, more vividly than my first pheasant or quail. I caught the frog in California, following instructions I'd read in a pamphlet. It happened in 1960, but the pamphlet went back to a time during the Second World War when the government published stuff meant to entice beginners, and maybe transplanted city folk, into harvesting wild things for food, to be combined with the produce of Victory Gardens. I don't know how helpful this was in releasing part of the national food tonnage for shipment to the armed forces, but it must have taught a few civilians new things to do with their time in the days when gasoline as well as food was rationed.

The recommended technique was really a crude form of fly-fishing, and what cruder fly-fisherman was there in 1960 than myself?

The fly was a one-inch square of red flannel. I guess you were supposed to snip it from your transplanted wife's country-style nightgown, so I doubt the piece I used was authentic. To turn it into a fly you just stuck a hook through the middle, rigged it on the end of fifteen inches or so of line tied to a cane pole, and dangled it in front of a daytime frog.

So equipped, except that I used my actual fly rod in place of the pole, I went out into a field late one afternoon, located a small pond where the frogs were singing, and crept up on it, ready to dangle. But I didn't creep so good the first time, and all the frogs saw me and jumped into the water.

While they were submerged, I found a little pondside hillock on which to lie on my stomach, fairly well concealed, and within a rod's length of the bank. And it wasn't long before the green ones started coming out to resume "Sweet Ranadine," and yes, there was a good big baritone almost directly in front of me.

So I inched my rod his way; since he was, of course, facing the water, I managed to loft the red tag over him from behind until it was dangling in the breeze four or five inches in front of his eyes. Damned if he didn't leap for it almost instantly, without leaving the bank, and take the next dangle firmly in his mouth.

I struck, hooked him, and had a lot of wiggle going on out there. Horsed him in, seized him, whacked him over the head with my sheath knife, and there was frog one.

Frog two never happened. But I did manage to kill, gut, and skin out the first one's legs, and we had one each (adults only) for hors d'oeuvres with that evening's martinis.

More civilized drinks were to follow, down the years, along with more elegantly caught frogs. For I must tell you that I didn't take to that method of frogging. That guy out there at the end of the rod, with his little arms, big legs, and baffled expression was too animal—even humanoid—and not enough fish. Didn't like it any better than I would have liked dangling a baited hook out in front of a rabbit hole. And anyhow, neither my pamphlet nor, subsequently, any of my sporting goods catalogs, had rabbit flies to offer.

Love,
Dad

. . .

Homestead, IA

Dear Dad,

Okay, I will follow your lead and stick with the subject of frogs for now, leaving for a time unput all the questions I am itching to ask: How many gators did you catch? How many of you did the gators catch? And so on.

Instead, let me consider the frog question for a moment and say that, despite having all the frogging opportunity a guy could want, I have not speared, hand-caught, or fly-rodded a frog in quite some years. I stopped looking at frogs with thoughts of eating them, I'm sorry to say, right after the last time you made frog legs for me. On that occasion the legs were not the crunchy, golden brown, garlicky, eat-them-like-potato-chips frog legs you'd always made before, but a sodden grayish mass, tasting not unlike frog-flavored oatmeal. I have been pretty much off frog ever since.

In fairness to you, however, I must admit that my indifference does not stem solely from one unfortunate dinner. My problem with frogging is not that frogs are too animal-looking or adorable to spear or catch. Quite oppositely, I find that, for some reason, the homelier the critter is, the worse I feel about killing it. Obviously I would make a very bad Cajun. I can stick my arms elbow deep into a deer carcass to pull out entrails that look just like mine without qualm or queasiness. I could probably shoot a unicorn if someone told me the chops were good and the population was up. The goggling frog, the gasping catfish, even the comical woodcock (which I hunt hard despite my misgivings about killing them), however, all provoke deep feelings of unease, when it comes to killing and eating them, that the dispatching of more attractive creatures does not. So, no frogs for me. Go figure.

Love,
Philip

. . .

Baton Rouge, LA

Dear Philip:

Sorry about that messy mess of frog legs. I'd happily forgotten but am now vividly reminded of how they looked—and there is no firmer believer than myself in the adage "The eye tastes first." I just checked a couple of cookbooks, and apparently what I was trying to do was produce *Grenouilles à la Provencal*, which are sautéed rather than fried deep in batter. I probably didn't get the pan hot enough.

Larousse Gastronomique, one of the books consulted, remarks, "It is well known that froglegs are not appreciated in England," and my advice to you is to forsake your limey ways in this area. And get the pan good and hot.

I finally did find a way of hunting frogs I thought was fun, and I wouldn't mind going at it now if I was on the farm.

However, before we moved to the farm, I went frogging with people fairly often in more conventional ways. The hunts took place at night. We generally went to that little two-acre body of water on County Road O called Swan

Lake—and if there was a ballet about that one, they'd have to costume the dancers as coots—but it sure had frogs.

We'd go by boat, wearing headlamps and wielding three-pronged gigs. The frog's eyes would gleam in the light; you could tell how big one was by how far apart the twin gleams were. Then you'd paddle as quietly as you could into gigging range, impale the frog, and transfer it into a gunnysack.

Got a lot of frogs that way, ate 'em crisp and garlicky, but still didn't like the blood or the fact that a gigged frog still has a lot of life in it.

Then along came John Yount, hero of so many of my letters, and he taught us that you can leave the gigs at home and get frogs into the gunnysack by whacking them with the flat of your hand, then closing the fingers around the slightly stunned frog. My only objection now was that when you got home with two or three dozen frogs at midnight, you were up till one or two in the morning, killing frogs and skinning legs.

There was one memorable night when we'd been especially successful, stayed out quite late, and John offered to take the frogs home and deal with them in the morning. He went back to his married-student-housing apartment, put the gunnysack with forty-five or fifty frogs in it in the laundry room in the basement, and went wearily to bed. In the morning he called me.

"I hope you weren't planning on frog legs for lunch," he said. "That gunnysack came open during the night, probably from the frogs moving around inside. Anyway, I've just come in from the yard, and every kid in Hawkeye Court's got him a pet frog this morning."

We moved quite far from Swan Lake when we bought the farm. I started building ponds, and we soon had our private frog supply around the edges of them. They were out, booming along, day and night, and I watched hungrily but still didn't feel like going back to gigging or even slapping.

Then one day I was out target shooting with that fine little .22 revolver—is it with you? Walking back, I went by the schoolhouse pond and saw six or eight good-sized frogs on the banks. I got down on my hands and knees, crawled to within ten or twelve feet of a nice, big frog, aimed at it with the handgun, and laid it out. Apparently the shock and concussion were as effective as the wound, and before the frog started to reflex I had him pan-ready.

It became something I did quite often when the weather was right, maybe because frogs were the only thing I could ever hit with a handgun other than a target.

Shall we now, as I continue to review notes and gather my energy to write my gator report, consider turtles, snapping? They were a quarry I pursued rarely, respectfully, and almost always in the knowledgeable company of Bohemian turtlers. Where are turtles, snapping, on your scale of homeliness, and the accompanying degree of reluctance to dispatch?

Love,
Dad

. . .

Homestead, IA

Dear Dad,

"The eye tastes first, but the stomach remembers." And, yes, my stomach remembers those frog legs. Vividly. To this day they strike a feeling of gastrointestinal terror in the pit of my belly matched only by the tremor I get remembering the *Fish à la Carbon Monoxide* I ate at a roadside restaurant in Greece. The kitchen sat on one side of an incredibly busy highway, the tables on the other, and the waiters risked their lives (and mine, as it turned out; I was sick for four days) dodging back and forth through clouds of exhaust fumes and speeding cars to bring us our food. Look that one up in your *Larousse Gastronomique*.

At any rate, to continue following this framework you insist upon, I will now turn my attention to snapping turtles, a subject about which I can, oddly enough, hold forth with some authority, having learned from the best. My turtle teacher was, as was yours, a Bohemian—what Cajuns are to Louisiana, so Bohemians are to eastern Iowa—Vern Zach. My education began about ten o'clock one summer Saturday when Vern pulled into my driveway unannounced in a converted Jeep with a canoe on top and two German shorthairs in the back. The dogs, it turned out, were not part of the turtling operation. I think Vern just put them back there so people seeing the Jeep would know whose it was. He handed me a beer and a tomato from his garden, which I accepted dutifully, assuming them to be somehow necessary to whatever was slated to follow. What followed was turtling, which turns out to be a two-day affair. (I'm speaking here only of summer turtling. On winter turtling, more later.) What we did was float around the pond in the canoe, tying short lengths (2–3') of stout string to the handles of empty milk jugs with the tops screwed firmly on. At the other end we fastened hooks, big ones, say ²/o or ⁴/o, and baited them with pieces of beefheart. We then had another beer and tomato each, floated around the pond wishing we had remembered fishing rods, then put the canoe back on the Jeep.

Next day, about the same time, Vern returned, same Jeep and canoe, probably different dogs—it's hard to tell, he has so many and they all look alike. I don't remember if we had more beer and tomatoes, but I suspect we did. I do remember quite clearly what we did next, which was to take the canoe back out on the pond and pull up our jugs, three of which had snapping turtles attached. I'd always known, sort of, that there were snappers in the pond, although it never really kept me from dangling my toes in the water or wading in old tennis shoes for bass. The sight of that first turtle, 35 pounds of hissing, indignant saurian, was enough to make a guy think about doing all his future swimming in steel-toed boots. My job was to handle the gunnysack, which I did, holding it wide open while Vern dropped the turtles inside. Vern told me not to get careless and sit too close to the sack, as friends of his had been bitten right through the burlap by bagged turtles in the past. I was very careful, and Vern quite competent from long practice, so that the only slightly dangerous moment occurred when we retrieved the jug from which a turtle had wrapped the line around a snag. Instead of picking up the jug, Vern had to reach underwater and grope around, untangling the turtle. This he did, pausing at one moment with the savoir faire of a man about to pull a rabbit from a hat to look at me, smile, and say, "I sure hope this is the right end," before hauling the turtle out of the water tail-first.

With our catch of two large turtles of about 35 pounds and a smaller 10-pounder stowed in the gunnysack we repaired to the barnyard for turtle butchering, which was, in a way, the most amazing part of an eye-opening experience. First it was remarkable because Vern, while professing not to be an expert like some guys he knew, had these three turtles taken apart and ready for cooking in a matter of minutes. I wouldn't even have known where to start. Second, it was amazing because the turtles, who date back to a time when life was much simpler than it is today, seemed to view being cut up as only a minor inconvenience. One of the disjointed feet grabbed ahold of the pliers in my hands and wouldn't let go. The head continued to hiss and stare balefully long after it was severed from the body, and the heart, which Vern cut out and set aside, *wouldn't stop beating*.

I jugged for turtles a time or two by myself after that, with moderate success, and on the question of whether turtles are too homely to kill, they are, but there's a him-or-me aspect to having an angry snapping turtle in a canoe with you that makes it a little easier to ignore your feelings of sympathy and whack him over the head pretty fast.

Turtling, I've since learned, is a year-round sport for the committed, many of whom actually prefer to turtle in cold weather. Although I haven't yet done it myself, what it takes is a steel rod four or five feet long with a hook on one end.

What you do is walk along the banks of a creek, poking the pole in the mud, looking for turtles burrowed underneath it, which is where turtles go when it's cold. A *clang* means you've hit rock, while a *thunk* signifies turtle. Often a *slurp* precedes the *thunk*, which is the sound of the air escaping from the burrow—"Breaking the seal" is what turtlers call it. You then turn the pole around and use the hook end to latch on under the shell and pull the turtle out of the mud. I'm told they are a good deal more sluggish and less likely to take off a finger in cold weather. The hard-core turtler, by the way, will turtle all winter, so long as he can find open water.

And now, having delivered the turtle story apparently required of me in order to learn about alligator hunting, there it is, and will you please get on with it.

> Love,
> Philip

. . .

Baton Rouge, LA

Dear Philip,

Here we go. Gator day was pretty fascinating.

I'd expected to be called out for one of those predawn starts familiar to duck hunters, infantrymen, and a certain percentage of hardy trout fishermen, but when I phoned the evening before, Bobby Guste said, "Come about nine."

This isn't to say that Bobby himself hadn't seen the sunrise, only that he was letting us off that part of it, when the hooks are baited and the lines set.

He also said, "Never mind the boots," for he'd told me when we first discussed the hunt that I'd need hip boots. I learned later that he was letting me off something more arduous than early rising.

So, at 8:30 on a gorgeous, hot September morning, I picked up Jon Kemp, who was lending her decorative, nature-loving presence and through whom I'd met Bobby in the first place.

Among the several grandsons of the family that owns Antoine's restaurant, Bobby is the outdoor guy, slight, strong, bristling with energy, somewhere in his thirties, and good fun to be around.

I'd been to his place once before, and it's extraordinary—many thousand acres of marshland alongside Lake Pontchartrain, opposite New Orleans, with a little farmland here and there. When there was farming, Bobby was the farmer. When there were crawfish ponds to farm, Bobby raised the mudbugs. There was always prime duck-shooting for the family and friends, and Bobby attended to that, too. Now much of his place is run as a duck club, and naturally Bobby manages that, and has recently started up a shooting preserve for quail and chukars. He has a pen of European wild boars he's raising and occasionally conducts hunts for the wild boars still out in the woods. And for one pretty stressful month of the year, he harvests alligators.

He lives by himself in a one-room cabin on the land, is cheerful and unpretentious, drives the obligatory beat-up pickup, smokes a lot, and when I hefted the unpretentious gun we were taking along and asked, "Are you loaded?" I got the answer I deserved:

"No," Bobby said. "But I will be along about seven o'clock this evening."

This battered gun, by the way, was a .22 magnum, hardly the bear-and-elephant rifle I'd been expecting.

With it we three climbed into the truck and Bobby drove us off over a bumpy dirt track to where one of his aluminum boats was moored. Yep, the boat was unpretentious, too, what we used to call a johnboat in Iowa, with a smallish outboard motor. The rest of the alligator hunter's equipment was a pair of canoe paddles, seat-cushion life jackets as required by law, half a broomstick with a hook fastened to the end (I'm not sure what for), the gun, and a big cooler full of Diet Coke.

We pushed off, settled ourselves, and paddled out, pushing

aside tree branches, into water deep enough to lower and start the motor.

Again, the unexpected: I'd been thinking bayou, but this was an old, man-made canal of still, opaque water. Though we saw members of the heron tribe from time to time, along with crows and blackbirds, it was too late and too hot for a lot of bird action, but the wildflowers along the banks were spectacular, if unidentifiable for Jon and me.

Big, yellow single blossoms on tall bushes, even bigger pink blossoms, and plants that bloomed in lush, red clusters among the reeds and marsh grasses. The smell of mud: duckweed drifting in green specks. I think Jon had just re-marked sentimentally that it sure was peaceful when Bobby cut the motor and we glided up to a piece of white line, not much bigger around than a kite string, tied to the trunk of a small tree and going from there diagonally into the water. It was very still, but we could see that it was in tension, and Bobby said:

"We've got one on."

Jon and I shifted, nervously if you like, but at least to be sure to be out of the way.

Bobby took hold of the line, and as soon as he tightened it, there was a good deal of underwater turbulence on both sides of the boat. This localized on the port side as he moved his quarry over and started hauling up.

The nose, hooked lower jaw, and eyes of an alligator appeared beside us, above the surface. Then the tail came thrashing out of the water, and whacked the side of the boat. The head, fully emerged, banged into us, too. It was not as large a head as I'd anticipated, maybe eight or ten inches across the brow, but certainly toothy enough to have bitten a medium-size dog in half, not to mention detaching a human forearm or leg.

The next thing the alligator did was spin. The whole creature straightened out from head to tail, and went whirl-ing around on the axis provided by the hook and line. Bobby was grinning, but he was holding hard, too, getting the head immobilized against the side of the boat. When he'd done that, he held the line with his left hand, picked up the gun with his right, held it centered on the gator's head an inch or two away, and fired. The bullet went straight through the skull and out the throat; so much for elephant guns.

As a veteran decapitator of chickens and, in my boyhood, rattlesnakes and copperheads, I expected prodigious reflex action, and again was wrong. This creature thrashed a time or two, subsided, and Bobby let go of the line so that the gator drifted back down.

We'd haul him in on the way back, rather than letting the carcass ride around with us in the hot sun.

Well, I thought, very interesting, not so hazardous after all. It wasn't until a couple of days later that I heard about a counterpart of Bobby's who, on hauling a big gator out of the water, had it take a big enough bite out of the aluminum boat to swamp it. As they struggled in the water, the hunter did manage to shoot his quarry a couple of times and make it to the bank. But I'm pleased that I hadn't heard the tale on gator day.

What happened next was not much for a while, but pleasant. We motored along, checking lines every couple of hundred feet without seeing another one stretched down into the water. The hooks are baited with day-old chicken breast, bone-in—I mean, we're not planning to make Chicken Kiev. They are big hooks, maybe an inch and a half across, silver colored, and are hung straight down from a limb, held to it by a clothespin. When the bait is taken, the pin snaps away. The end of the line is tied to the trunk of the tree, often a pretty small one.

"As soon as the gator gets back in the mud, he feels pretty safe," Bobby said, and explained that the hooks are hung about 18 inches above the water so that the smaller alligators can't reach them.

Two good reasons: An alligator less than four feet long

must be released. In addition, we were engaged, really, in a commercial harvest, and the bigger the beast, the better the price. The hides are worth $40 a foot currently. The meat, sold mostly to restaurants, brings $4 a pound. The gator we'd just killed was about six and a half feet. It would fetch somewhere around $350, whereas one eleven to twelve feet long would be worth a thousand.

These prices were low, Bobby told us as we motored from line to line. The market had been weakened by the sale of a lot of farm-raised gators, though the farmers routinely slaughtered them at four feet. Couldn't afford to feed them up any bigger than that. And it turned out Bobby himself had helped to create the competition: for several years, in the spring, he'd made a business of hunting alligator eggs. This had its own kind of hazard—you didn't want a big old female to see you robbing her nest as you waded around clumsily in hip boots.

He'd incubated the eggs, hatched them out, and sold the babies to the farmers. Wasn't doing it anymore. Poor market there, too. Farmers were going broke. Hey, the ostrich farmers in Louisiana were having a rough time, too.

What is it you guys farm in Iowa? Hogs and corn?

There were no more hooked gators in the first canal we ran. It was a canal he was trying out, and it was proving unproductive.

We headed back, pulled the dead alligator into the boat, and Bobby made a slit in the tail through which to fasten a tag.

We went back to the mooring to drop off that first alligator in the cool of the cabin and went on to another johnboat moored in another canal.

Did better in that one: four more alligators, one of them an 8-footer. We could, actually, have had five, but Bobby felt one of them, and a very lively one at that, was undersized and cut him loose, severing the line with his clasp knife just outside the mouth.

"Will the hook work itself out?" I asked, knowing it happens with fish.

"A gator's blood is so acidic that if you have a cut on your hand and get gator blood in it, it'll sting for an hour. Anyway, it'll melt the barb off the hook in three or four weeks."

"I'd think he'd have trouble eating, though."

"Well, I'll tell you this. When one's been dead a day or two, he'll swell up and float. I've never found one floating that way that had a hook in its mouth."

Then he explained the hunter's quandary: he gets a tag for each 200 acres he owns, leases, or has permission to hunt on. Bobby himself had 70 such tags, and 30 days in which to use them. At the rate of that day's harvest, he could have had all his tags on in a couple of weeks, but the only reason to do it would be if a cold snap were predicted, which would send the reptiles down for the winter. Otherwise, keeping the smaller ones meant sacrificing chances for big ones. And finally, the bureaucratic fly trap: You were supposed to keep every gator you hooked, right? But you must cut loose any under four feet, right? Keep your knife sharp.

Wait, did I say one tag per 200 acres? And that Bobby had 70 tags? That does make 14,000 acres, doesn't it? Cripes. Some of them he hunts on foot, in boots, finding potholes at which to rig lines. Often the holes are made by the gator itself; they enlarge as the creature grows, and often it spends its whole life there. It was hot, sweaty work hunting those places; you had to be quick.

"When you get him up, he'll spend a few seconds looking at you. That's when you have to shoot him or he'll haul ass, and since you're on foot, if he's big you may have to let go."

It was lunchtime when we got back to the cabin, loaded up our five gators, and collected seven more Bobby had stored in a big freezer. We were going to Licata's with them. In the backroom at Licata's, which is also a pretty nice restaurant, gators are bought and measured prior to processing.

"They'll razz me," Bobby said. "These are pretty small. Did I tell you 90 percent of the ones we get are male?"

There was a 12-footer on the table in the room, which did make our bunch look small.

"How do you sex them?" I asked.

Bobby put his finger in the vent of the big one and said, "This here's a male. You can feel the penis."

I put my finger in and could feel it readily, a sticklike affair with a sort of swollen hook on the end. Jon sexed the gator, too, and Bobby offered to cut the member out. It could be dried as a souvenir. I declined, but I'm not sure why. It would have made an interesting lamp pull.

The restaurant, where we had lunch, reminded me of something far away in time and place, but I'll need three or four more paragraphs to suggest what and why.

There are, at Licata's, a couple of tables off to the side, where the alligator men sit together when they come in to eat. Vincent Licata, the proprietor, hunts too. Vincent came over and joined us when we sat down. He features alligator soup on his menu, and I'd ordered a cup. Very good, much like the turtle soup that you recall, with chunks of somewhat chewy meat and hard-boiled eggs cut up in it.

"We throw the meat in the stockpot with vegetables and cook it all day long," Vince told me.

As we talked about the big, 12-foot gator in the back and other related matters, we were joined by and heard shoptalk from another hunter. I waited until there were just Jon, Bobby, me, and our beer glasses, then asked Bobby what had been his closest call.

"It was the biggest gator I ever caught," he said. "Twelve and a half feet and six hundred pounds. When I pulled him up, I was standing at the end of a ten-foot boat. He went down, the line caught across the boat, and he pulled that end under. I managed to get back to the other end, slipping and sliding, so we stopped taking water, and then I had to use a come-along, a hand-winch, to pull him in."

The place I was reminded of was a restaurant we used to go to in Mexico City, forty years ago. It was where the bull-fighters hung out at special tables, and we knew some of them well enough to sit with them sometimes. I don't suppose the connection's hard to see.

Love,
Dad

Chapter 14

BOOKS

Homestead, IA

Dear Dad,

I was looking through some stuff I used to think I couldn't live without and getting rid of it the other day, when I came across the salmon fly from Roderick Haig-Brown you gave me, along with a letter he sent to you about it, it being the "Old Gammarus Fly." Not knowing what else to do with an old Gammarus Fly, I donated the fly and letter to the American Museum of Flyfishing in Manchester, Vermont, which I hope you'll agree is a good place for them. The folks at the museum seemed to think so, but then they would, wouldn't they?

I looked up *gammarus* in the dictionary, but unfortunately my Random House skips straight from *gamma ray* to *gammer* without pausing to explain what any kind of gammarus, old or new, might be. The letter from Haig-Brown to you suggests you were writing an article for the *New Yorker* about salmon flies at the time. That would make you an expert, so you can tell me what a gammarus is and put my mind at ease. Meanwhile, I think I'll see if I can't dig up your old copy of *A River Never Sleeps* and finally read it. I've been meaning to for years, but never have. Finding the fly and reading the letter have put me in a mood to read the book.

Love,
Philip

. . .

Baton Rouge, LA

Dear Philip,

The other day in the hallway of the English Dept. I asked my colleague Gale if he could remember the name of a particular student who'd been here five years ago.

"It's too recent for me," I said. "If it were fifteen or twenty years ago, I'd remember easy."

Gale, though he's not quite as old as me, said he knew exactly what I meant and couldn't recall the guy's name, either. So I asked a much younger colleague and got it—though the outcome has nothing at all to do with why I'm describing the incident.

I'm describing it because I recall that when R. Haig-Brown sent me that fly, about thirty years ago, he remarked that the *gammarus* was a freshwater shrimp. According to one of my dictionaries (a stout one, the three-volume *Webster*), he was wrong. The *gammarus* is crustacean all right, but the examples are the sand flea and the whale louse, neither of which sounds as if it would be any good boiled, chilled, and served with cocktail sauce. That's all the dictionary cares to say about the creatures, except for some confusing discussion of mandibles and thoraxes.

But how big, do you suppose, is a whale louse? Maybe with the right kind of cocktail sauce . . .

Anyway, I'm glad you found the Haig-Brown book, which is a nice one and which probably has something to do with why, at the time, I kept on writing hunting pieces until I had enough of them for a book of my own. It seemed that, with one exception, the literature of fishing was held in greater esteem than works about hunting, and I found that a challenge.

The one exception was Hemingway's *Green Hills of Africa*, and even that mighty writer's fishing stuff—like "Big Two-Hearted River"—seemed to be preferred. However, *Green Hills* is nonfiction about hunting and to my mind a hell of a book. Have you read it?

The reason why fishing works offer elegant prose, I would guess, has to do with the British stereotype of the fly fisherman, a civilized, elitist, contemplative fellow sucking on an unlit pipe. I suppose the stereotype led those in its image to write about fishing as the outdoor sport of the reflective man—but as noted previously about freshwater fishing, the chief reflection associated with it in my mind is that of my face in the water as I'm about to fall into it.

Anyway, there are some good fishing books in that collection I left behind at the farm with you (hey, Ray Bergman's *Trout*, which you mentioned earlier), and a wonderful hunting book, though it wasn't written in English, Turgenev's *A Sportsman's Notebook*. Which op. cit. Hemingway loved a lot. Sometimes I miss those books.

But other books do keep coming. I've just read one you sent me, as a matter of fact—*Lone Tree*, about the murder of everybody in our part of Iowa's favorite banker, John Hughes. And there are catalogs to wish through, and then it will be spring.

Love,
Dad

. . .

Homestead, IA

Dear Dad,

Thanks for answering the gammarus question, and also for raising another in its place—that is, why fishermen are thought to be more sensitive prose stylists than hunters. It would be disingenuous, I think, not to suspect a certain amount of anti–blood sport sentiment here. There is writing about bird hunting every bit as good as the best fishing stuff, and *Green Hills of Africa* could well be the best sporting book of them all, its politically incorrect author and topic notwithstanding. Me, I always thought fishing was a blood sport, too: killing is killing, serious business regardless of whether the quarry is trout or kudu. Mine, however, seems to be a minority opinion.

Curious that you should mention Turgenev since I got a letter from a guy last fall asking if he could stay with me and hunt pheasants as part of a nationwide research trip for a book about bird hunting in America. The project, he claimed, was inspired (sort of) by *A Sportsman's Notebook*. Later he sent me a postcard from West Virginia explaining that he was mired knee-deep in grouse and wouldn't be able to make it out here before pheasant season closed. Tough job, huh? Why didn't I think of this one first? Obviously because I haven't read my Turgenev. I'll find it and read it after I'm done with the Haig-Brown.

Love,
Philip

. . .

Baton Rouge, LA

Dear Philip,

You're into some long books, so we'll make this a short letter, but here is something that fascinates me about *A Sportsman's Notebook*, which was Turgenev's first. It's credited with having had the same effect in Russia on the emancipation of the serfs that *Uncle Tom's Cabin* had on the emancipation of the slaves over here. The *Notebook* was read apparently by everyone in Russia who was sufficiently literate, including the tsar. Its description of the conditions in which the serfs lived and the cruelties to which their owners subjected them seems to have put into words what everybody knew but didn't want to think about. Turgenev knew about the cruelties firsthand—his mother, a big landowner and serf-holder, was one of the beastliest. People hued and cried; the government acted.

What fisherman's book ever made that kind of history?

Love,
Dad

.   .   .

Homestead, IA

Dear Dad,

This discussion of outdoor books that began with flies reminds me, naturally, that I have been hanging on to the enclosed wood-duck lemon feathers since last fall. I've been meaning to ask you for John Yount's address; I wanted to send him the feathers as you used to so he could turn them into Hornbergs.

Like most of the ducks I kill these days, this one was more or less an accident. Sam and I were out pheasant hunting when I spotted some woodies on the creek. Hoping to catch up to a straggler, I broke into a run, tripping on some rusty barbed wire at streamside. There was one duck who was slow to flush, rising off the creek as I was falling toward it. I killed him with my second shot.

I did not, however, land in the creek as you would have done, although I didn't stay dry for long. Sam ran down the bank, tested the depth and temperature of the water gingerly with one paw, and scrambled back up—wading is one thing, he decided long ago, but swimming is simply not in his job description. So this duck hunt ended like so many of yours did, with a dripping hunter turning blue, clutching a bedraggled duck in one hand, pulling himself out of the creek bed with the other, pretending he's having fun. Explain to me sometime exactly what it is you miss about it.

Nevertheless, here are the feathers for you to forward to

John, who belongs in this correspondence anyway, along with your other students—Tom Williams, Dick Wentz, and Charles Gaines—who taught you to hunt and fish while you were teaching them to write.

Love,
Philip

. . .

Baton Rouge, LA

Dear Philip:

The lemon feathers are on their way to John. There will be Hornbergs. But I didn't realize until the last line of your letter that you didn't know Tom Williams had died in New Hampshire last October.

God, what a beautiful month October is in New England.

I've been wanting to write something about Tom, to whom I was very close for a long while, and from whom I never felt distant even when we'd put too many miles between us to see one another much. I hope it's appropriate to write it here.

Do you remember him? When you were a little guy in North Liberty, years ago, you were with Tom and me in a pasture. He and I were taking turns with a hand trap, throwing clay and shooting. I had put my 12-gauge aside empty, thrown a couple of birds for Tom, and when I picked up the gun again you scooted over to the ammo supply and brought me a 20-gauge shell.

"I think he wants to blow you up," Tom said, but he said things like that with a twinkle in the bright, attentive eyes behind his glasses. Made me laugh, and I think you understood from his manner that you might have made a mistake but you weren't going to be thrown out of the fraternity for it.

Tom was a graduate student in the Iowa Writers Workshop then, but he'd already published *Ceremony of Love*, his first novel, before he came to Iowa, and some of the other students had at least mild feelings of hero worship toward him. But it wasn't just because of the writing. He was strong and graceful, around six feet, I guess, with thin blond hair—I once heard him described as "a great muscular cat."

All one fall Tom and Dek Lardner and I hunted birds together. In the winter Tom and I taught ourselves to play squash (and did it almost every day). We sat in on the same quarter-limit poker game every Friday night and in the spring played softball, poets vs. fiction writers, if we didn't go trout fishing. I'd say he taught me to flycast if I were any good at it; better to say he watched me trying to follow his instructions with tolerant amusement. I've got to add that I held my own on the squash court, but he was a good outdoorsman, a hell of a writer, and devastating at seven-card stud, high-low, aces swing, and chips declare.

He'd grin that grin as the final round of betting started and say, "I'm going to enjoy this. I've got locks," but you never knew whether it was high or low.

Got him good once. I'd been missing Tom a lot when he finished in Iowa City and moved on to the University of New Hampshire, on whose letterhead came a request that I recommend him as a Ph.D. candidate. I wrote a strongly favorable letter, of course, but then retyped it in such a way as to produce what appeared to be a carbon copy for Tom, to which I added the line: "He is, I must say in all candor, a little quicker than he needs to be at yelling 'I got him' when we both shoot at the same duck." Tom couldn't be sure whether or not to believe my forgery, and I let him wonder for a while, but I also took to visiting him in Durham and in his woods camp whenever I went east, and there was always some sort of outdoor stuff to get into together.

At the camp, very deep in the woods, Tom and Liz designed and built their own cabin, but it wasn't a cabin. It was a lovely, sturdy house of logs and glass and stone. I remember watching him put logs in place with block and tackle and heft stones salvaged from an old New England wall. He loved physical work and had the combination of skill and strength to do it smoothly and well.

A year or two after he'd been appointed to the UNH
English faculty, Tom asked me to suggest someone to join
him there as a writing teacher; I sent him John, my next close
student friend. I was seven years older than Tom, and probably twice that many older than John, but it pleases me to say
that they always treated me like a contemporary.

I sometimes felt a kind of squash-court rivalry with Tom
about writing. Even before he left Iowa, I had to admit to
myself that he was a better hand than I at the short story. Tom
wrote one back then called "The Goose Pond," which Rust
Hills published in *Esquire*, and which has made a lot of anthologies since. You and I have been corresponding about
outdoor literature, but without saying much about fiction. So
far as a short story with hunting content goes, "The Goose
Pond" would be on anybody's best 10 list. You can find it in
one of my favorite of Tom's books, a novella and story
collection called *A High New House*.

. . .

Well. Our children grew. I remarried and relocated. Didn't
see much of my old New Hampshire friends for maybe a
decade, but the last time I did see Tom—about five years
ago—he was still fine and twinkling. He was worried about
Liz, who'd broken a leg skiing and was having mending
problems. He was pretty much nursing her. She had to wear a
brace to play tennis, and I recall Tom's saying it was important to him that she have as many years possible of doing
her kind of outdoor things, which she loved as much as he
did his.

Then, a couple of years ago, I had a call from John and
learned that it was Liz who was doing the nursing—the
profession she was trained for, actually—and Tom who
needed it now. It was lung cancer, and he was so strong
physically that he didn't show many symptoms until the stuff
had spread all through him: liver, lungs, stomach, every-
where.

Yep. He smoked. (So does that other marvelous physical specimen, John, and I wish to hell he'd quit.)

Three things kept Tom going: his strength, Liz's nursing, and an experimental chemotherapy program at Dartmouth that kept losing people, but not old Williams. He and Liz fought the cancer; I phoned one Sunday, and he had a lot of self-mocking things to say about the way his hair was falling out and so on. Then, when I phoned again last spring, he said he was in remission; they might have got it beat, and that his hair had grown back "a funny color." He expected to be teaching again in the fall and was looking forward to it a lot.

But, of course, he didn't teach again. Damn stuff recurred. He was pleased, though, that his publisher planned to get some of his books back in print, and not long before he went out he said to Liz (so she told me), "It's okay, I've made my peace."

Tom left eight novels, the novella-story collection I mentioned, and had won a National Book Award. He was wonderful at making images; he'd studied painting before he decided to write. I think it takes someone with a painter's eye to use words with the precision he does in this passage (from his novel *The Followed Man*):

> [Luke Carr's Uncle Shem's possessions included] . . . a large jackknife with staghorn handles smoothed by use down to the ivory, its largest blade honed narrow. Luke could hear Shem telling him that the blades were called clip, sheepfoot and spay, and that the knife "walked and talked" which had to do with how healthy a click the blades made when opened or shut. Back when Shem showed it to him, Luke's fingernails were not large enough or strong enough to dig into the blade knicks and open it. But now they were and it still walked and talked.

So does Tom's prose and so, for his friends, does Tom.
                                        Love,
                                        Dad

Epilogue

___

As a child, what I wanted to be more than anything was the kid on "Flipper." I carried a big, hardbound book called *Living Fishes of the World* around with me the way other children carried blankets. When I got a little older I snorkeled in our ponds. I'd catch the occasional glimpse of a drab bass scooting into the weeds, and once I tried some unsuccessful spearfishing, too, with a frog gig. My parents, bless them, indulged me with a couple of skin-diving trips to the Caribbean and, once, an afternoon of deep-sea fishing off Acapulco.

I still have *Living Fishes of the World*, I'm still landlocked in Iowa, but, thanks to my father's letters, I've gone along on fishing trips from Maine to India, in fresh and salt water both. In fact, given the way my adult stomach reacts to the motion of a small boat, it may be more comfortable for me to do my fishing from my living room, anyway. Actually, if there were a way to fax fillets, fishing by mail might be better than the real thing.

It's hard to feel sorry for myself for living in Iowa. The closest ocean may be a thousand miles away, but in the spring I've watched cock pheasants strutting ten steps from my front door, and sometimes in the fall I've had to hold my fire to keep from blowing out my kitchen windows as I flush those same roosters from the cornfield behind the house. There are deer nearby in the creek bottoms, turkeys and mushrooms in the woods, a surprisingly good woodcock flight most years, and a handful of grouse, partridges, and quail for variety. You will not catch me complaining—not, at least, from mid-October to the end of December, nor again in April and May.

The outdoor life I'm living now is not too different from the one my father enjoyed so much when he was here. He left it behind several years ago, and I know he misses it very much. I also know that he wanted me to share his passion for the outdoors and, especially, bird hunting with him. I'm glad we're finally able to do that now, albeit belatedly, and by mail. I hope he's pleased that the upbringing he gave me finally took and that I derive as much pleasure from hunting as he used to.

I remember his writing in *Country Matters* that when I was young he imagined our hunting together when I got older, back on the home place. We'd ride on horseback, following a pointing dog or two, shotguns in saddle scabbards, an idyll I shattered by refusing to hunt at all.

I think I remember Dad shooting cap pistols near the horses at feeding time to accustom them to gunfire. I may be inventing that memory, but I did find the scabbard, still unused, in storage a few years ago. I cleaned it up and gave it to Vern Zach, who wanted it for field trialing.

The hunt on horseback was Dad's dream hunt with me. I'll tell you now about my dream hunt with him. It, too, takes place on Redbird Farm, because hunting on his own land was what Dad liked most of all. Down on the creek bottom, where the loggers didn't cut, we now have wild turkeys, thanks to restocking by the Iowa Department of Natural Resources. In fact, the turkey release took place up on the hill near the one-room schoolhouse Dad used as a writing studio.

I'm sorry he wasn't there to see the birds released; that was exactly the kind of project he loved.

The turkeys have multiplied and spread up and down the creek. Only a few have stayed on our place, but I've shot a gobbler in almost exactly the same spot three years in a row, just across the creek, south of my mother's house. I'd like to take Dad down there and call one in for him. I know it would be more of a thrill for him to see a turkey on the farm than to shoot one anywhere else. And I'm pretty confident we wouldn't just *see* a turkey down there—I think I could get him a shot. Frankly, I'd also enjoy the chance to show off to my dad a little; I'm no longer the novice whose letters you read in the earlier chapter "Turkey Season."

We may never get together for this hunt any more than we ever hunted quail together on horseback, but here's how I imagine that morning: We'd be up early, well before dawn, crossing the old iron bridge across the creek in full darkness. I'd be in the lead, shining a pocket flashlight on the bridge planks so Dad could avoid the holes I've already committed to memory. He'd be carrying my turkey gun, a 12-gauge Browning pump, which I'd have covered with an extra layer of dull camouflage tape, both to hide it from the turkeys and to protect the finish from Dad, who's hard enough on guns in broad daylight. We'd turn right, walking to the end of the vacated road, then out along the edge of the sandy cornfield on the south side of the creek. At the field's edge there's a steep drainage ditch to clamber across, then we'd be in the woodlot. Quietly I'd show him to the huge old locust tree near the turkey's favorite roost. (I'd have checked the night before, waiting until dusk to watch the tom fly up, then tiptoeing away under cover of darkness, to make sure he was in his usual tree.)

I'd take a minute to clear the dead branches away from the base of the tree so they wouldn't rustle and snap if Dad moved. Then I'd nervously whisper some meaningless last-minute advice and sneak back the way we'd come to take a seat against another tree about twenty yards behind the locust. I'd settle in on the seat cushion and get my calls ready. First I'd chalk the box call and set it down with the lid open wide so it wouldn't squeak when I picked it up. I'd put the slate call on my lap, and rough up the surface with a scouring pad. One diaphragm call would go in my mouth; the other would be close to hand in one of my vest pockets.

As the sky lightened to the west, we'd hear owls, then crows, cardinals, wood ducks, and, finally, a hundred fifty yards ahead of us, a loud gobble. I'd smile behind my face mask, wondering if Dad was as excited as I was the first time I heard a gobbler sound off. After a few minutes, I'd try some soft yelps, holding the slate cupped in my right hand, making small circles on the slate with the striker held in my left hand like a pencil. The bird would gobble back. I'd wait ten minutes, call again, then put the slate back in my lap.

Shortly after dawn we'd hear the turkey fly down, loud wing beats carrying the heavy body to the ground. He'd gobble on the ground, and I'd answer with a string of five eager yelps on the box call, my tone conveying rising urgency. He'd gobble back again. Perhaps he'd even double gobble (since this is my dream hunt and my dream turkey, he can be in a mood to make me look *very* good if I want him to). Then I'd catch my first glimpse of the tom, strutting toward us seventy-five yards away, his fan tilting back and forth, catching the morning sun. I'd shut up then and make him look for me. He'd come in, alternately craning his neck up high to search for the phantom hen, tucking it against his breast to strut, then thrusting it straight ahead and gobbling.

My part would now be over, except to watch and listen anxiously for the sound of the shot when the bird stepped into range. And, if Dad found the bird too startlingly beautiful to shoot and let it pass by unharmed, as I know he might, it really wouldn't matter at all.